THINKING OUT LOUD

A program of activities for developing speaking, listening and thinking skills for children aged 8–11

BY LYN DAWES, NEIL MERCER AND RUPERT WEGERIF

ACER Press

Adapted and published 2006
by ACER Press
Australian Council *for* Educational Research Ltd
19 Prospect Hill Road, Camberwell, Victoria, 3124
by arrangement with Imaginative Minds
1st Floor Leonard House
321 Bradford Street
Birmingham B5 6ET, UK

First published 2000
as *Thinking Together: A programme of activities for developing speaking, listening and thinking skills for children aged 8–11*

Copyright © 2006 Lyn Dawes, Neil Mercer and Rupert Wegerif

Selected pages from this book may be photocopied for use by the purchaser or purchasing institution only. Otherwise all rights are reserved. Except under the conditions described in the Copyright Act 1968 of Australia and subsequent amendments, no part of this publication may be reproduced, stored in a retrieval system or transmitted in any form or by any means, electronic, mechanical, photocopying, recording or otherwise, without the written permission of the publishers.

Copyright Permission
Open All the Cages © 1992 Richard Edwards
From MOON FROG by Richard Edwards, illustrated by Sarah Fox-Davies
Reproduced by permission of Walker Books Ltd, London SE11 5HJ

Every effort has been made to acknowledge and contact copyright owners. However, should any infringement have occurred, ACER tenders its apology and invites copyright owners to contact ACER.

Printed by Shannon Books

National Library of Australia Cataloguing-in-Publication data:

Dawes, Lyn.
Thinking out loud: a program of activities for developing speaking, listening and thinking skills for children aged 8–11.

For primary school children.
ISBN 9780864315816.

ISBN 0 86431 581 3.

1. Language arts (Primary) – Activity programs. 2. Listening – Study and teaching (Primary) – Activity programs. 3. Critical thinking in children – Study and teaching (Primary) – Activity programs.
I. Mercer, Neil. II. Wegerif, Rupert, 1959– . III. Australian Council *for* Educational Research. IV. Title.

372.6

Visit our website: www.acerpress.com.au

Contents

Introduction to the Australian edition — iv

How and why to teach the Thinking Out Loud lessons

The aims of *Thinking Out Loud* — vii
The principles of *Thinking Out Loud* — vii
What makes the lessons work? — viii
Assessing progress — xi
Links to Australian Curriculum Frameworks — xiv
The sections of *Thinking Out Loud* — xx

Section A Focus on Talk

Lesson 1 Talk about talk — 2
Lesson 2 Talking in groups — 8
Lesson 3 Deciding on ground rules — 12
Lesson 4 Using the ground rules — 19
Lesson 5 Reasoning with ground rules — 23

Section B Talking, Thinking and Learning

Lesson 6 Persuasion — 32
Lesson 7 Kate's choice — 36
Lesson 8 Who pays? — 40
Lesson 9 Water voles — 48
Lesson 10 Town plan — 64
Lesson 11 A fair test — 69
Lesson 12 Non-fiction — 72
Lesson 13 Looking into poems — 77
Lesson 14 Staying friends — 80
Lesson 15 Strategy — 84
Lesson 16 ICT and learning conversations — 86
Talk certificates — 89

Introduction to the Australian Edition

Thinking Out Loud is the Australian edition of a thinking skills program from the United Kingdom known as 'Thinking Together'. ACER Press is pleased to make this highly successful UK program available for an Australian audience. Some modifications have been introduced, including a new section providing an overview of thinking skills in Australian curriculum frameworks and some minor adjustments to language and terminology.

The teaching of thinking is seen as a very important goal of education in the twenty-first century. The key features of the emphasis on thinking skills might be summarised as follows:

- Explicit attention should be given to the development of thinking skills.
- Students should be encouraged to think about thinking and to develop metacognitive skills.
- Learning to think involves the investigation of discipline-based methodologies and reflection on their usefulness in different contexts.
- Discriminating thinking about controversial and complex issues is at the centre of learning to think.
- Learning to think involves students reflecting on their own and other people's values.

The teaching of thinking can play a central role in educational programs by integrating different subject areas and integrating the development of cognitive skills with the development of personal values.

Thinking Out Loud is a set of 16 lessons designed to develop thinking skills through 'exploratory talk'. The lessons aim to explicitly encourage the use of ground rules for effective talk as the basis of group work in all curriculum areas.

Lessons 1 to 5 focus on talk itself. Children are encouraged in these lessons to become more aware of the ways they talk together, and they are given the task of establishing explicit ground rules for talk. In lessons 6 to 16 students apply the ground rules in problem solving and collaborative learning activities related to different subject areas. Each lesson includes worksheets and suggestions for adapting and extending the activities.

Thinking Out Loud integrates the development of speaking and thinking skills through collaborative activities. In doing so it picks up the emphasis on generic communication and thinking skills in contemporary Australian curriculum documents. The approach and the activities in *Thinking Out Loud* also reflect the growing emphasis on 'essential learning' in Australian curriculum documents by integrating the following kinds of key skills and thinking skills:

INTRODUCTION

Key skills
- Communication
- Working co-operatively with others
- Improving own learning and performance

Thinking skills
- Information processing
- Reasoning
- Problem solving
- Inquiry
- Creative thinking
- Evaluation

An overview of thinking skills in Australian curriculum frameworks has been provided on pages xiv–xix.

Editor's Note:

Some consideration was given to modifying Lesson 9: Water voles due to its UK-centric content. However, it was decided that the lesson as it stands is an effective teaching and learning activity. In addition to the generic skills and strategies developed in the activity, Australian students will need to develop their capacity to think about issues outside their normal environment, and apply thinking processes to other, less familiar environments. In particular it will require students to develop some specific understanding of UK ecology, variations in climate, and different animal species.

Teachers who would prefer to set the activity in a more familiar environment could adapt it themselves. See the list of conservation issues under 'Extension work' on page 49 for ideas.

HOW AND WHY TO TEACH THE THINKING OUT LOUD LESSONS

THE AIMS OF THINKING OUT LOUD

Thinking Out Loud is based on the successful UK thinking skills program called 'Thinking Together'. The *Thinking Out Loud* activities included in this book are designed to develop the speaking, listening and reasoning skills of children aged 8–11 and have been shown to improve their educational achievement. Activities are included which relate to most curriculum subjects as well as English.

The activities are organised into a series of lessons, each of which provides resources for organising whole-class and group activities in ways that have been shown to improve the quality of children's talk and their active participation in class. The activities:

- raise children's awareness and understanding of their use of spoken language
- help them communicate and work together more effectively in groups
- improve their critical thinking skills

The relationship of the contents of the *Thinking Out Loud* lessons to various Australian curriculum frameworks is discussed on pages xiv–xix.

See also the website which provides more information about the *Thinking Out Loud* approach, including comments from teachers and examples of children working together: www.thinkingtogether.org.uk

THE PRINCIPLES OF THINKING OUT LOUD

Thinking Out Loud materials are based on research carried out over several years by a team based at the Open University. This applied research has been supported by the Economic and Social Research Council, the Citizenship Foundation, the Nuffield Foundation, the Esmee Fairburn Trust and by Milton Keynes LEA and other local educational authorities. The research showed that by using some practical, down-to-earth strategies and activities, teachers could enable children to become significantly better at talking and thinking together. Children were then able to apply these skills in their study of the curriculum. One of the most striking findings was that children not only became better at thinking together but also on their own. That is, the research provided clear evidence that there is a link between the development of children's language skills and the improvement of their critical thinking. Thinking together, out loud, is good preparation for thinking alone.

The *Thinking Out Loud* approach was first implemented in primary and middle schools in south-east England, where teachers worked closely with the researchers in the development and testing of classroom activities and teaching strategies. It has since been successfully implemented in other parts of the UK and in other countries such as Mexico and Holland. Its findings have been incorporated into National Strategies for education in literacy and the foundation subjects in the UK, and the value of the approach is recognised internationally.

Exploratory Talk

A key element of the *Thinking Out Loud* approach is the concept of Exploratory Talk. Exploratory Talk happens when people engage critically but constructively with each other's ideas. This means that:

- everyone shares relevant knowledge
- contributions are actively sought from each participant
- challenges and alternative proposals are accepted, but must be justified by reasons
- agreement is sought and achieved wherever possible.

When children are using language in this way, their reasoning becomes visible in the talk—for example, in their frequent use of words like ' I think…' 'because…' and 'why…?'. This kind of rational discussion is of great value in education. Through engaging in Exploratory Talk, children learn to develop their own ideas and learn from those of others. They also learn skills in talking and thinking which enable them to work more effectively in teams and to take an active role in society. Exploratory Talk is a very intimate way to talk to other people, in that it allows access to what other people really think; it is also quite impersonal, in that it can take place between any group of people, even complete strangers.

However, research has shown that in most primary classrooms—anywhere in the world—hardly any Exploratory Talk normally takes place. The quality of much group work is unsatisfactory and fairly unproductive, with children not really grasping how they are expected to work together. They rarely have the principles of effective co-operation in small-group situations explained to them, or have effective strategies for thinking together explained by their teachers. The *Thinking Out Loud* materials were created to improve this situation.

WHAT MAKES THE LESSONS WORK?

The success of the *Thinking Out Loud* program is in the hands of the teacher. The main points to bear in mind when using the lessons are as follows:

Establishing 'ground rules' for talk

In each lesson, the teacher sets up a situation in which children solve problems together. During the first three lessons, the children are guided towards formulating some straightforward ground rules for talking together. If followed, these ground rules ensure that the children begin to use Exploratory Talk. All voices are heard and all points of view are supported by reasons. Members of a group are expected to seek agreement before taking a decision. This means that no individual can be made to feel they have caused the group to do something 'wrong', and no individual can claim credit if things turn out right. The effects of the *Thinking Out Loud* activities on children's educational progress will be strongest if they are explicitly encouraged to use the ground rules in all group work, across the curriculum.

How and why to teach the Thinking Out Loud lessons

Making the aims for each lesson clear

The plan for each lesson sets out particular aims or learning intentions for the children's work together. These are not written in 'child-friendly' language because the lesson plans are for teachers, not children, to read. One of the most important aspects of this approach is that as each lesson starts, the teacher shares the learning intentions for talk with the children. This helps to establish a joint purpose for each activity, and keeps the focus firmly on the talk. Any reading, writing or drawing the children do is incidental. The children should be aware that they must concentrate their greatest efforts on the way they are talking to one another.

Combining whole-class and group activities

Good practice in classroom education is not a matter of choosing between teacher-led, whole-class teaching and group-based activities. Both of these ways of organising teaching and learning have their value. Effective teaching depends on organising a suitable balance between whole-class and group-based work. The *Thinking Out Loud* lessons have been designed to help you achieve this kind of balance. Each lesson has three main sections:

WHOLE-CLASS INTRODUCTION in which the teacher:

- explains the aims of the lesson
- talks about the main themes with the class
- sets up the group work session.

GROUP WORK in which the children work together on an activity in their 'talk groups'.

WHOLE-CLASS PLENARY is a session in which the teacher:

- enables the groups of children to share their work with the class
- leads a class discussion to draw out the main points that have emerged
- reviews the aims for the lesson with the children to consider if they have been fulfilled. This discussion allows the children to evaluate the process of thinking together, so that they become more aware of the power of productive talk to help their individual reasoning and learning.

Each lesson is a self-contained, integrated set of whole-class and group activities. Suggestions for possible extension work are included in the lesson plans. Displaying work, or reading and writing activities stimulated by the talk, may be best kept for separate sessions so that the talk activities retain their strong focus on spoken language and reasoning.

Making the most of group work

Children may never have thought about the ways they talk together and how some ways of communicating can make group activities more productive and enjoyable. They may need help to learn how to use spoken language effectively. As educators, we may not have made clear what we want and expect when we ask groups to 'discuss' or 'talk together to decide'. Group activity is likely to be productive and fulfilling if:

- all members of the group take an active part
- everyone's ideas and suggestions are accepted openly for consideration
- everyone accepts that their ideas can be questioned
- everyone gives reasons to support their objections and proposals
- members of the group take joint responsibility for decisions.

Not only does this kind of communication generate better group activity, it can also help individual children to improve their 'critical thinking' or reasoning.

There are many factors to be taken into consideration when dividing the class into groups for the *Thinking Out Loud* lessons. Some points to note are:

- Groups of three provide a varied source of ideas without there being too many voices to be heard. Groups of four tend to split into two pairs, and pairs may not be able to generate discussion as readily as threes.
- Friendship groups may not produce the most effective way of working. Friends working together tend to agree with each other's suggestions without critical consideration.
- It is important that each talk group contains one child who can read and write reasonably well, so that any written instructions and other materials are properly understood. The program is designed to allow children of different literacy abilities to contribute on as equal a footing as possible.
- Mixing boys with girls in groups may allow more opportunity for creative friction and for developing children's abilities to work co-operatively with a variety of partners.
- Having constructed a list of children in each group, it is helpful to talk through your reasons with the class, stressing that people have been allocated to groups for positive reasons such as: having good general knowledge; being a good listener; being good at asking questions; being thoughtful; being good at including others; being good at reading, writing, using a computer and so on.

In summary, we have found that groups for these lessons are best made up of three children of mixed ability, male and female, and with all individuals distributed to help encourage reluctant participants and avoid serious personality clashes. However, grouping classes is a subtle process in which the teacher's understanding of the people in class is critical. You may have occasion to group in friendship groups, groups of four, and so on for various reasons.

Using appropriate teaching strategies

The success of the *Thinking Out Loud* approach depends on teachers taking a leading role in guiding the development of children's language use and understanding. This will include:

- making the learning intentions for each activity clear
- regularly reminding children to use their 'ground rules' for talk
- 'modelling' for children the kinds of language they should use to talk to one another in groups. For example, teachers can ask children 'Why?' and 'How?' questions during whole-class sessions, or as they monitor group activity. This helps children to reflect on what they think they know, and to put their reasoning into words
- using questions not just to test children on specific items of knowledge, but using a series of related questions (perhaps involving several children) to lead children through a line of reasoning. So, for example, the teacher asks for one child's ideas, and then asks other children to build on this contribution in a way that helps the entire class to come to a joint understanding of a topic. This kind of 'whole-class dialogue' creates a bridge between whole-class activity and group work
- helping children recognise and value the language and reasoning skills they are developing—for example, children can consider whether using the ground rules is improving how they talk and work together. The review of learning intentions at the end of each lesson can also help to consolidate children's learning.

ASSESSING PROGRESS

The *Thinking Out Loud* lessons provide excellent opportunities for assessment because the teacher inevitably listens to groups and individuals and collects information about the development of children's competence, understanding and skills. The focus may not just be on individuals' skills in speaking and listening but also on their study of other curriculum subjects. Opportunities will arise to check for misconceptions and gaps in understanding. Intervention—to challenge misconceptions, restructure understanding and provide further information—can then be accurately focused. This process allows the teacher to adapt what is planned to meet the needs that are identified.

The questions for teacher assessment listed below can be used in formative assessment. How the questions are used will depend on a teacher's particular aims or concerns. You may wish to concentrate on particular children who you suspect have difficulty in speaking and listening, or to survey the talk of the whole of the class.

Assessing children's talking and thinking together during group work:
1. Does the child initiate and carry on conversations?
2. Does the child listen carefully?
3. Can the child's talk be easily understood?
4. Can the child describe experiences?
5. Can the child give instructions?
6. Does the child follow verbal instructions?
7. Does the child modify talk for different audiences?
8. Does the child ask questions?
9. Does the child give reasons?
10. Does the child ask others for their views?
11. Does the child reply to challenging questions?
12. Can the child take joint responsibility for decisions?
13. Can the child 'think aloud'?
14. Can the child generate and consider an alternative point of view?

Self-evaluation by children during plenary time

Each lesson has evaluation opportunities as part of its plenary. The list of plenary questions below suggests some ways in which children can be helped to reflect on the quality of their talk:

- How did the ground rules help you to talk about this activity?
- Evaluate the reasons offered. Which was the most valid?
- How did sharing your ideas help to develop your thinking?
- How did sharing your ideas help your group to reach a decision?
- Did your group reach a decision? Did the ground rules help you to do this?
- What were other possibilities? Why did your group reject these?

Self-assessment: Talk Diary

A Talk Diary can be used to build up a more comprehensive picture of talk awareness. This can be completed at the end of each lesson or intermittently to suit your purposes. Talk Diary is a suggested format: children can tick boxes, or enter a score out of ten.

TALK DIARY

Name: _____ Start date: _____

	Thinking Out Loud lesson numbers				
	1	2	3	4	5
I talked in the whole-class session					
I talked in a group session					
I asked a relevant question					
I answered a question or challenge					
I gave a reason for my ideas					
I explained what I thought					
I listened actively					
My group talked well					
We used Exploratory Talk					
I contributed information					
I used the ground rules with a group at the computer					
I learnt or understood more from talking to my group					
I found it difficult to talk					
I found it hard to listen without getting distracted					
Our group could not agree on a joint decision					
We decided together					

Thinking Out Loud   Copyright © 2006 Dawes, Mercer and Wegerif

Links to Australian Curriculum Frameworks

The last decade of the twentieth century and the beginning of the new century has seen growing interest in Australia and other countries in the generic skills of literacy and numeracy, and in general thinking skills. The National Goals for Schooling in the Twenty-first Century identified by the different ministers of education in Australia in 1999 gave particular emphasis to the generic thinking skills of analysis and problem solving. The idea that Thinking Skills are essential learnings has been given a good deal of attention in various curriculum documents in recent years.

The approach and the activities in *Thinking Out Loud* reflect this growing emphasis on 'essential learning' by integrating the following kinds of key skills and thinking skills:

Key skills
- Communication
- Working co-operatively with others
- Improving own learning and performance

Thinking skills
- Information processing
- Reasoning
- Problem solving
- Inquiry
- Creative thinking
- Evaluation

The following is an overview of thinking skills in the curriculum frameworks of Australian states and territories.

New South Wales

In New South Wales the following generic skills have been identified in K–6 syllabus documents.

Skill Focus	Description
Research	Locate, select and evaluate information from a variety of sources
Communication	Present and communicate information according to purpose, situation and audience
Solving Problems	Apply a range of problem-solving strategies to achieve an accepted solution
Using Technology	Select and use the most appropriate technology for a given task
Critical Thinking	Make personal judgements and informed choices
Task Management	Use time and resources effectively
Cooperation	Work cooperatively with others
Citizenship	Develop an awareness of personal, local, national and global responsibilities
Expression	Respond emotionally and imaginatively through creative and expressive activities

Source: <http://k6.boardofstudies.nsw.edu.au/linkages/Generic/mapping_generic_skills.pdf>.

Queensland

In Queensland the notion of Rich Tasks was developed. In these tasks students could demonstrate 'understandings, knowledges and skills through performance on transdisciplinary activities that have an obvious connection to the wide world'.
Source: <http://education.qld.gov.au/corporate/newbasics/html/richtasks/richtasks.html>.

Rich Tasks are the assessable and reportable outcomes of a curriculum plan that prepares students for the challenges of life in the future of increasing globalisation with 'constantly changing technologies, complex transformations in cultural and social relationships, fluid demographics, and a sense of uncertainty about the future'.
Source: <http://education.qld.gov.au/corporate/newbasics/html/curric-org/curricorg.html>.

The Rich Tasks require students to solve problems, be critical and analytical thinkers, and use the knowledge and skills they have acquired, in a variety of contexts in a variety of ways. They also require students to tie new learning to what is already known, to have a clear statement of expectations and realise that their knowledge can be transferred to new situations.
Source: <http://education.qld.gov.au/corporate/newbasics/html/richtasks/richtasks.html>.

South Australia

The Essential Learnings developed in South Australia describe the need for students to 'develop a sense of the power of creativity, wisdom and enterprise and capabilities to evaluate and generate ideas and solutions'. The curriculum developed from the Essential Learnings provides learners with opportunities to 'think about thinking'. By developing a range of 'systematic, logical, innovating and rigorous thinking and action processes', it was intended that 'learners would be able to solve problems creatively and generate solutions'.

Source: <http://www.sacsa.sa.edu.au/index_fsrc.asp?t=EL>.

Thinking and the thinker were described in the following terms in the Essential Learnings of South Australia.

THINKING
Knows self profoundly as a thinker and learner
Is a critical thinker
Is a risk taker
Is imaginative and creative
Presents particular points of view
Advocates for strong beliefs or values based positions
Can draw on thinking from different times and cultures eg holistic systems, thinking of Buddhist culture
Thinks expansively
Can critically reflect
Seeks a range of perspectives
Plans and organises events and learning experiences
Knows there can be more than one right answer
Experiments with ideas
Gathers evidence to support arguments
Generates ideas
Thinks about how they are learning and using thinking processes to learn
Consciousness about the world views that influence their own and others' thinking

Source: http://www.sacsa.sa.edu.au/ATT/%7B02BAFA66-6D7E-4597-8CBA-3DF370C0DF1D%7D/EL%20Concise.pdf

Northern Territory

The Essential Learnings developed in the Northern Territory described an 'Inner Learner' who would be a self-directed and reflective thinker.

Inner Learner "Who am I and where am I going?"	A self-directed and reflective THINKER who
	In 1 Uses own learning preferences and meta-cognitive processes to optimise learning.
	In 2 Identifies and actively develops their natural talents, self-worth and learned skills to pursue and achieve their personal goals.
	In 3 Makes decisions and takes actions based on personal values and principles that reflect empathy and integrity.
	In 4 Assesses their well-being and takes action for healthy living.
	In 5 Demonstrates resilience in pursuing choices and dealing with change.
	In 6 Explains how the past, present and future contribute to their own identity and broaden life directions.

Source: http://www.deet.nt.gov.au/education/ntcf/docs/b_essential_learn.pdf

Western Australia

The Core Shared Values developed by the Curriculum Council in Western Australia encourage each person 'to reflect critically on both the cultural heritage and the attitudes and values underlying current social trends and institutions'.

Source: http://www.curriculum.wa.edu.au/support/cd/CF/fwk13.htm

Tasmania

The Essential Learnings Framework developed by the Tasmanian Department of Education has thinking (inquiry and reflection) at the centre of four related sets of considerations:
- Communicating
- Personal futures
- World futures
- Social responsibility.

See the link below for a representation of Essential Learnings Framework 1:
<http://www.ltag.education.tas.gov.au/ELsresources/overviewintro.pdf>.

Thinking is seen as having two key elements in the framework:
- inquiry
- reflective thinking.

Inquiry is understood to be based on:
- posing problems
- gathering information
- thinking about possibilities
- making decisions
- justifying conclusions.

The following key questions about the process of inquiry are posed for educators:
- What skills and attitudes of mind are required to pose and define problems, clarify the issues involved and select and modify processes to use for inquiry?
- How can learners gain the skills to identify their information needs and collect, organise and evaluate data?
- How can the capacity to consider new possibilities and create new solutions be developed as a natural part of inquiry?
- What is required for learners to be able to evaluate the benefits of proposed solutions, uncover underlying assumptions and assess risks and limitations?
- What does it mean for all learners to explain and justify conclusions in a fair-minded way?

Reflective thinking is understood to be based on:
- thinking about thinking and learning
- understanding and caring about different perspectives
- ethical reasoning.

The following key questions about the process of reflective thinking are posed for educators.
- What can assist learners to think about, describe and improve their thinking and learning?
- What skills, knowledge and dispositions are required to consider different perspectives, manage disagreement productively and accommodate alternative points of view?
- What are the principles of ethical decision-making, and when and how can they be applied appropriately to life questions and issues?

Tasmania has offered standards for Thinking. These can be viewed at:
<http://www.ltag.education.tas.gov.au/ELsresources/outcomesandstandards.pdf>.

Victoria

The Victorian Essential Learning Standards involve interdisciplinary knowledge, skills and behaviours in:
- Communication
- Design, Creativity and Technology
- Information and Communication Technology
- Thinking.

The Victorian Essential Learning Standards encourage:
- discriminating thinking about controversial and complex issues
- the cognitive, metacognitive and affective elements of thinking
- the investigation of discipline-based methodologies and to reflect on their usefulness in different contexts.

The discriminating thinkers envisaged in the Victorian Essential Learning Standards will select and use thinking processes and tools appropriate to particular tasks, and evaluate their effectiveness. They will:
- develop questioning techniques and generate questions that explore differing perspectives;
- probe into and elicit information from varying sources
- process and synthesise complex information
- identify assumptions that may underpin a particular line of reasoning
- make informed decisions based on their analysis of various perspectives and, sometimes contradictory, information.

Discriminating thinkers are envisaged as able to:
- reflect on their own thinking and identify assumptions that may influence their ideas
- use specific language to describe their thinking and reflect on their thinking processes

- explain conscious changes that may occur in their own and others' thinking and analyse alternative perspectives and perceptions.

The standards envisage that discriminating thinkers will:
- analyse the relationships between ideas, and synthesise these to form coherent knowledge
- investigate a variety of discipline-based methodologies and reflect on their usefulness in different contexts
- explain the different methodologies used by different disciplines to create and verify knowledge.

VELS has six levels of student achievement in the Thinking Processes domain. These can be viewed at:
http://vels.vcaa.vic.edu.au/downloads/vels_standards/velsrevisedthinkingprocesses.pdf

Web links

New South Wales
Board of Studies, K to 6
http://k6.boardofstudies.nsw.edu.au/

Queensland
Department of Education and the Arts
http://education.qld.gov.au/

South Australia
South Australian Curriculum Standards and Accountability Framework
http://www.sacsa.sa.edu.au

Northern Territory
Department of Employment, Education and Training
http://www.deet.nt.gov.au

Western Australia
Curriculum Council
http://www.curriculum.wa.edu.au

Tasmania
Department of Education
http://www.ltag.education.tas.gov.au

Victoria
Victorian Curriculum and Assessment Authority
http://vels.vcaa.vic.edu.au

Australian Capital Territory
Department of Education and Training
http://www.det.act.gov.au

Thinking Together
www.thinkingtogether.org.uk

THINKING OUT LOUD

THE SECTIONS OF THINKING OUT LOUD

Thinking Out Loud is intended as an approach to teaching and learning as well as a set of specific activities. The benefits of *Thinking Out Loud* lessons on educational progress are most noticeable where children are explicitly encouraged to use ground rules for effective talk as the basis for group work in all curriculum areas. The lessons suggested here are examples of the *Thinking Out Loud* approach which may inspire you to make your own adaptations and to develop the approach throughout the curriculum. The *Thinking Out Loud* lessons are divided into two sections.

Section A: Focus on talk

These first five lessons aim to encourage children to become more aware of the ways they talk together. Students are given the task of establishing specific ground rules for talk. Each lesson focuses on a different ground rule or sub-component of effective *Thinking Out Loud*, such as accurate listening, asking questions or giving reasons. These lessons could be used in the first week of a new school year to create a climate of collaborative learning in the classroom—or perhaps to start a new term with a new approach. The five lessons in Section A are:

LESSON 1: TALK ABOUT TALK
LESSON 2: TALKING IN GROUPS
LESSON 3: DECIDING ON GROUND RULES
LESSON 4: USING THE GROUND RULES
LESSON 5: REASONING WITH GROUND RULES
EXTRA LESSONS: THERE ARE TWO OPTIONAL EXTRA LESSONS, 2A AND 5A

Section B: Talking, thinking and learning

The lessons in this section build on the skills and understanding developed in Section A. In Section B, children apply the ground rules for thinking to problem-solving and collaborative learning in different curriculum areas. It will be assumed that shared ground rules have been established in the class, so it is important to complete all of the Section A lessons first.

The ground rules are used throughout this section, but each lesson also highlights specific ground rules and aspects of thinking together. These will be explained in the lesson aims. As with the lessons in Section A, there are worksheets and suggestions for adapting or extending the activities. Here is a brief outline of each lesson.

LESSON 6: PERSUASION. This provides three contexts in which children are required to use persuasive reasoning. First, the children practise using persuasive vocabulary and then write a persuasive letter. Finally, a short drama activity allows the groups to share their understanding of the powers of persuasion.

Lesson 7: Kate's choice. Children practise reasoning together in the area of citizenship, with a computer program providing a context and prompt for reaching joint decisions. This lesson provides a template for using computers to encourage and support thinking together.

Lesson 8: Who pays? This builds on Lesson 7 to give children further opportunities to apply the ground rules in trying to resolve a moral dilemma. A short story entitled 'Who pays?' is used to encourage children to make joint decisions and present their ideas as a group.

Lesson 9: Water voles. The board game focuses on the plight of one of Britain's most endangered species, in order to encourage children's critical questioning and reasoning. Groups make joint decisions and present their ideas together.

Lesson 10: Town plan. Children are asked to design a new town and must collect and share information with their group. This develops their ability to provide clear instructions, act upon them, and make joint decisions.

Lesson 11: A fair test. Using the context of a science investigation into materials, the children talk together to define a hypothesis and plan a 'fair test'. The groups are required to make joint decisions and present their agreed ideas.

Lesson 12: Non-fiction. Children use the ground rules for talk to discuss a non-fiction text. Whole-class work provides a structure for this activity, in which groups work collaboratively on reading for meaning.

Lesson 13: Looking into poems. Children study three poems together in this lesson, which provides opportunities for critical thinking. Individuals are required to justify their opinions with reasons.

Lesson 14: Staying friends. This lesson offers an additional citizenship context for practising the ground rules for talk. A short story provides the basis for discussion about which choices are available and why.

Lesson 15: Strategy. This lesson is another variation on the game of Battleships. It aims to encourage collaboration in pairs, with children accepting responsibility for joint decisions.

Lesson 16: ICT and learning conversations. Using ICT, co-operation between children, both face-to-face and at a distance, is established. The activities enable children to share relevant information, and to create resources together by communicating their ideas effectively. Children are encouraged to use the computer as a communication tool.

Structure of the *Thinking Out Loud* lessons

The *Thinking Out Loud* lessons in both sections are designed to teach ground rules for encouraging Exploratory talk. In Section B, it will be assumed that the class has agreed on a set of ground rules for talking together, which will be displayed prominently in the classroom, and referred to frequently.

These lesson plans can be used as a template for developing further lessons. Suggestions of how to do this are included, along with photocopiable worksheets. Each *Thinking Out Loud* lesson plan has the following structure:

RESOURCES. Materials needed for each activity are listed here, including the photocopiable activity sheets contained in this book.

AIMS. One critical aspect of the *Thinking Out Loud* lessons is that, as each lesson starts, the teacher explains the lesson aims to the children. This helps to establish a shared purpose for each activity, and keeps the focus firmly on the talk. Any reading, writing or drawing the children may do is incidental. Students should be aware that they must concentrate their greatest efforts on the way in which they talk to one another.

WHOLE-CLASS INTRODUCTION. Each lesson begins with a whole-class session in which the teacher explains the lesson aims, talks about the main themes with the class and sets up activities. The introduction notes are intended for teachers' use, rather than for students, and are therefore not written in 'child-friendly' language.

GROUP WORK. During this phase the teacher asks students to join their designated 'talk groups'. The students will then work collaboratively on tasks in these groups.

PLENARY. The teacher brings the class together at the end of the lesson to:
- enable groups to share their work with the class
- lead a class discussion, drawing out the main points that have emerged
- review the lesson aims, allowing the class to decide whether they have been fulfilled.

This discussion can also be used by teacher and students as a means of informal assessment.

EXTENSION WORK. Some of the lessons include extra activities for the children to work on—either independently at the end of the lesson, or at home. There may also be suggestions for further lessons or reinforcement activities.

SECTION A
FOCUS ON TALK

Thinking Out Loud

1. Talk about talk

Lesson 1

Resources
Dictionaries, thesaurus, display materials
Worksheets: 1A: *A list of talk words*
                    1B: *Sorting talk*
                    1C: *Speech bubbles*

Aims
- To raise children's awareness of how they talk.
- To introduce some words for describing ways of talking and to enable children to practise using them.

Whole-class introduction
Introduce the new 'talk topic' and explain the aims for Lesson 1. Ask the children for their ideas about talk, using the following open-ended questions as a structure. These questions should elicit a range of contributions based on personal experience and ideas.

GENERAL QUESTIONS
Are you good at talking?
Do you ever get asked to stop talking? Who asks this? When?
Does anyone ever try to make you talk when you don't want to?
Do you like using the telephone? Who do you talk to?
Do you know anyone who is easy to talk to? Can you say why?

QUESTIONS ON LEARNING TO TALK
Has anyone got a baby brother or sister at home?
How do babies learn to talk?
Who taught you how to talk?
Do you learn how to talk in school?

QUESTIONS ON USING TALK
Are you asked to talk together in class? In which lessons does this happen?
Why is talking a useful skill? (Give reasons.)
What tasks can people get done by talking to each other?
How would you communicate with other people if you couldn't talk?
How many different languages can you speak?
How many different languages have you heard of?

QUESTIONS ON COMMUNICATING
What happens when people talk but others don't listen?
What are the differences between talking and writing?

SECTION A: FOCUS ON TALK

Group work

1. SORTING TALK

Provide each group of children with *Worksheet 1A: A list of talk words* and *Worksheet 1B: Sorting talk*. Ask the groups to talk together to put each word on *Worksheet 1A* into one of the boxes on *Worksheet 1B*. Tell them that they should:

- use a dictionary to clarify any unfamiliar words
- only write the words in, once the group has agreed
- find two new words to go into each box by using the thesaurus.

2. SPEECH BUBBLES

Provide each child with a copy of *Worksheet 1C: Speech bubbles*. Ask the group to:

- choose a word from the list on *Worksheet 1A*
- draw a cartoon and a speech bubble in the first box, to show the word being used
- write the word in the space below the cartoon
- pass the sheet to another group member until everyone in the group has drawn a cartoon on each sheet.

3. DISPLAY

Ask each child to draw a life-sized talking head with a large speech bubble, then write one of the talking words in it. These can be mounted to make a display. For class discussion, ask the children to share their completed work. Consider:

- When is it important to be silent?
- Why is silence important in some lessons?
- Do some people enjoy silence more than others?
- What has silence to do with thinking and concentrating?
- Can people talk and think at the same time?

Whole-class plenary

Ask the children to reflect on the session content and on the quality of their talk together:
How well did your group work together?
Did you use talk to get the group work done?

Extension work

- At home, children could ask parents or relatives to describe their experiences in classrooms—when was talk allowed, encouraged, or discouraged?
- Children could find out how old they were when they began to talk, and see if anyone remembers what they first said or recalls any amusing things that they said.

Lesson 1

- Children who can speak more than one language can be asked to contribute by describing how they choose which language to use when they are talking. What problems have they encountered? What problems have single-language speakers encountered in visiting other countries?
- Sign languages for the hearing-impaired can be studied.
- Children can find out about codes for communicating such as Morse code or semaphore. Dance or drama can be used to explain 'body language'—what are its limitations when compared to spoken language?
- If any of the class uses email to communicate with a friend, they could bring a printed sample to share. What are the similarities and differences between email, talking together, and writing to one another?
- Comics can provide a rich source of speech bubbles. In some comics, language is used creatively to convey sound or action. The class can draw cartoon characters with speech bubbles to convey the meaning of the words on *Worksheet 1A* for display.

SECTION A: FOCUS ON TALK

A LIST OF TALK WORDS

brag	reply
chat	tell
chatter	softly
conversation	stammer
demand	argue
dialogue	splutter
enquire	threaten
explain	screech
gossip	answer
laugh	natter
loudly	ask
moan	croak
mumble	grumble
mutter	dispute
persuade	reason
scream	request
shout	jabber
tell off	row
whisper	fiercely
yell	discuss

Worksheet 1A

Thinking Out Loud   Copyright © 2006 Dawes, Mercer and Wegerif

Worksheet 1B

THINKING OUT LOUD

SORTING TALK

- Talk **LOUDLY**
- Talk
- Talk quietly
- Talk *angrily*
- Question and answer
- Any other words

Copyright © 2006 Dawes, Mercer and Wegerif

SECTION A: FOCUS ON TALK

SPEECH BUBBLES

Cartoon	Word
Cartoon	Word
Cartoon	Word
Cartoon	Word
Cartoon	Word
Cartoon	Word

Worksheet 1C

2. Talking in Groups

Resources
Paper and pens, stopwatch or timer
Worksheet 2: Some starter questions

Aims
- To start children working together in talk groups and establish group cohesion.
- To help children practise taking turns in talk.

Whole-class introduction
Explain the aims for Lesson 2 to the children. Talk to the children about the criteria used to organise the groups. Explain that each group is a combination of these sorts of people:

- a good listener
- a good writer
- a person who has lots of good ideas
- a co-operative person
- a thoughtful person
- a confident person.

Explain that this means that friends will not always be working together, that the groups have been carefully chosen and are not negotiable. Hand out or display *Worksheet 2: Some starter questions*, and explain the task.

Group work

1. INTERVIEWING

Two members of the group have to interview the third about their favourite free-time activity or hobby. Nothing at all should be written down by the group at this stage. Display the prompt questions and explain that these are only suggestions—their own ideas may well be better. The interview will last one minute. Interviewers must listen carefully to the answers. After the first interview, the process is repeated with the other members of the group. If someone claims they have no interests, they should be asked to describe, in great detail, what they did the previous evening or weekend.

2. CLASS DISCUSSION

When the interviews are complete, the group talks together and appoints a speaker. Taking turns, the speakers from each group briefly describe the hobbies of the group members. Individuals may be asked to answer questions from class members.

SECTION A: FOCUS ON TALK

Next set up a class discussion, with the following suggested talking points:

- Why do you think teachers sometimes ask you to work in groups?
- Is it always easier to work with your friends?
- Do you like working in a group? Why/why not?
- Who do you think is a good person to work in a group with and why?
- What do you think are good rules for working together in a group? (Briefly—this will be developed further in Lesson 3.)
- If your group is trying to decide something, for example if you are using the computer and one person makes a suggestion, what should the other members of the group ask for before the suggestion is accepted? (The aim here is to encourage children to recognise the need for a reason.)

Whole-class plenary
Ask the children to reflect on the session content and on the quality of their talk together:
Can anyone give a good example of how your group took turns to talk?
Who have you talked to who is a good listener? How do you know?

Extension work
- Children can interview someone at home, or an invited guest from another class, about their hobby.
- The children can create a display board depicting their hobby, with a brief description, or use a 'question-and-answer' format to explain the activity. The talking groups can each be given a folder in which group work will be collected. Group members can discuss how to decorate this in a way that reflects their various interests.
- The class can begin a collection of pictures of people talking together from publications such as magazines and newspapers. For example, the pictures could include politicians, parents and children, children playing games or at the computer, or adults discussing things. The pictures could be used to create a display with captions. The teacher should use the display to stress the uses and purposes of talking together.
- If you feel it would be helpful, Lesson 2A: Building Copies (page 11) can be used at this stage to develop children's awareness and understanding of talk.

Some Starter Questions

What do you like doing in your free time?

Where do you go to do that?

What started you doing that in the first place?

Do you need special equipment or clothes?

Is it an expensive hobby?

How long have you been doing this activity?

What do your family think of it?

Who do you do it with?

What do you hope to achieve?

Do you ever get fed up and want to stop?

Do you think other people in this class would like to do it too?

What else do you enjoy doing?

2A. Building Copies

Resources
Two matching sets of construction material for each group (e.g. Lego baseboard and 10 Lego pieces)

Aims
- To help children give accurate instructions and ask relevant questions.
- To raise children's awareness of how they talk.

Whole-class introduction
Explain to the children the aims for Lesson 2A, then explain the following activity.

Group work
Two group members should sit back-to-back. One of them will make a model or pattern with their set of construction materials. Once it is complete, their partner must ask for instructions on how to build an identical model. Instructions can only be given in response to questions asked. The third group member observes and can make suggestions if the partners cannot resolve difficulties that arise. Once models are copied successfully, the partners change tasks within the group.

Whole-class plenary
Ask the class to describe the sorts of questions that provided useful information and the sorts of descriptions that were most accurate. Ask the children to reflect on the content of the session, and on the quality of their talk together:

How accurate were the instructions?
Did listeners ask relevant questions?

Extension work
A similar activity can take place using paper and pencil. One of the partners draws an object, then (without naming it) describes how to draw it.

Mathematical vocabulary for this sort of activity could be illustrated and displayed for use: left, right, angle, right-angle, arc, curve, cylinder, rectangle, rhombus, rotate and so on.

The activity could also be undertaken by talk partners using email.

THINKING OUT LOUD

3. DECIDING ON GROUND RULES

Resources
Dictionary, thesaurus

Information sheets   *3A: Ground rules for talk (for the teacher)*
                        3B: Are these useful rules?

Worksheets   *3A: Talking words*
                        3B: Our ground rules for talk

Aims
- To raise children's awareness of the value of their talk together.
- To clarify relevant vocabulary.
- To decide on a set of ground rules for talk.

Whole-class introduction
Explain to the children the aims for Lesson 3. Briefly introduce the concept of ground rules for social behaviour. These are basic rules which operate even though they may never be discussed or written down. For example, what do the class think are the ground rules for behaviour in a train (using mobile phones, running), in a shop (queuing, handling goods), at the cinema (talking during the film, where people sit relative to one another), at the swimming pool (showering before swimming, wearing a swimming cap), being a car passenger (giving directions, shouting).

Explain that in joint activities in class, people learn most if they discuss things. Usually the ground rules for discussion are taken for granted. In this lesson, the class is going to decide which rules will help people to get the best out of group work.

Use *Information Sheet 3B: Are these useful rules?* Ask individual children to read the 'rules' aloud. Ask the class to comment on whether each rule would help to encourage group discussion and learning. This sheet should not be handed out to the children.

Group work

1. TALKING WORDS

Provide each group of children with *Worksheet 3A: Talking words*. Ask the groups to talk about their understanding of what the words mean.

2. CREATING A SET OF GROUND RULES FOR TALK

This activity is crucial for effective group work. Ensure that the children are aware of its importance. Ask the children to think alone for a minute. Ask them to reflect on what they know about working in groups. What sort of rules would help everyone to get the most out of the talk? What are good ways to find out what other people think? What difference does careful listening make?

SECTION A: FOCUS ON TALK

Provide each group with *Worksheet 3B: Our ground rules for talk*. Ask the group to appoint a writer. Ask the group to talk together to create and decide on their six most important rules, remembering that the aim of these rules will be to ensure effective group discussion. Encourage the children to consider the reasons for their choices.

Whole-class work

Arrange a class discussion in which the groups share their rules and reasons for them. Start by asking one group for one reason. Record this on the whiteboard. Now ask the next group. Continue to build up a set of reasons by adding to and revising the list. Try to ensure that the rules are concise, there are no more than six rules and that none of the rules start with don't.

These ground rules for talk should reflect those provided in *Information Sheet 3A: Ground rules for talk* (for the teacher). They will be worded as original rules contributed by the class.

Encourage the class to decide to use these rules in their group discussions. The rules can be displayed prominently. Each child can be given a copy.

Restate the lesson aims and discuss with children whether they have been achieved.

Whole-class plenary

Ask the children to reflect on the session content and on the quality of their talk together:
How well did your group work together?
What difference do you think it will make if we all use our new ground rules for talk?

Extension work

Provide children with a printed copy of the rules to take home for discussion with parents. Ask children (in groups) to consider what ground rules for talk they think are being followed in other situations:

- friends talking
- in assembly
- in the cinema
- in class when the teacher is introducing a new topic
- in a science or maths investigation
- in an outdoor game
- in the corridors at school
- on the telephone
- talking to the middle school co-ordinator
- talking to a visitor to the school

What are the differences between these rules and the class ground rules for talk? The children should have the opportunity to consider the value of the class ground rules as a 'fair' means of sharing information, ideas and opinions, and as a way of trying to find out and understand other people's reasons.

Ask the children to collect an example of the ground rules in action over the course of a week. They can write down the context and what was said, or just try to remember it. For example, collect a use of the word 'because', an example of someone giving a reason, or an example of someone asking another person what they think.

SECTION A: FOCUS ON TALK

GROUND RULES FOR TALK

It is crucial for the success of the *Thinking Out Loud* lessons that each class agrees a set of ground rules for talk which encourages effective, reasoned exploratory talk.
The class ground rules should reflect these ideas:

1. All relevant information is shared amongst the group.
2. Assertions and opinions should be backed up by reasons.
3. It is important to challenge and discuss suggestions and opinions.
4. Alternative options are carefully considered before any decision is made.
5. Everyone in the group should be encouraged to speak by the other members.
6. Contributions are treated with respect.
7. The group should try to reach agreement.
8. The group accepts collective responsibility for decisions made and actions taken because of those decisions.

During Lesson 3 these points are converted into a clear and simple set of rules that the children can 'own', appreciate and follow.

The principles above may have to be disentangled from other rules for talk in class that children may have learnt, or at least heard of, such as, 'Don't interrupt an adult', 'Don't use bad language' and 'Don't talk in assembly'. Although useful, these rules are not relevant to the ability to sustain educationally effective discussion, with its focus on reasoned argument and shared information.

An example of ground rules produced by a Year 5 class:

Our Talking Rules
- We share our ideas and listen to each other.
- We talk one at a time.
- We respect each other's opinions.
- We ask each other to talk.
- We give reasons to explain our ideas.
- If we disagree we ask 'why?'
- We try to agree in the end.

Info sheet 3A

Are these useful rules?

1. The best reader should decide.
2. Ask everyone in turn what they think.
3. Ask for reasons why.
4. Challenge what has been said if you have a different idea.
5. If people challenge your ideas, you can give reasons for them.
6. Choose as quickly as you can.
7. Make sure you have thought of all the choices before deciding.
8. If a wrong decision is made, choose who is to blame.
9. If you hear a good reason, it's sensible to change your mind.
10. If you know something important, keep it to yourself.
11. If you want to be heard, shout.
12. Make sure the group agrees after talking.
13. Make up your own mind straight away and stick to it.
14. Respect other people's ideas.
15. The group tries to agree before making a decision.
16. The most talkative person should speak most.
17. The oldest person should start the talk.
18. There should be a leader and the group does what they say.
19. People your own age can't teach you anything.
20. Make sure everyone is asked what they think.
21. Look at and listen to the person who is talking.
22. You should only agree with people you know.
23. Talking together helps you think.

SECTION A: FOCUS ON TALK

TALKING WORDS

- Tell each other what these words mean.
- Use them in a sentence if it makes explaining easier.
- If anyone in the group doesn't know what one of the words means, use a dictionary or thesaurus.

Tick a word when you think all of your group can say what it means.

Group talk words	Tick
1. opinion	
2. agreement	
3. relevant	
4. argument	
5. assertion	
6. alternatives	
7. challenge	
8. discussion	
9. reason	
10. critical	
11. respect	
12. information	
13. idea	
14. share	
15. positive	
16. negotiate	
17. attend	
18. reflect	
19. consider	
20. joint decision	

Worksheet 3A

Thinking Out Loud   Copyright © 2006 Dawes, Mercer and Wegerif

THINKING OUT LOUD

OUR GROUND RULES FOR TALK
Our group's suggestions for ground rules for talk

OUR NAMES	
Suggested rule	Reason why this would help us to learn better in a group
1	
2	
3	
4	
5	
6	

Our group thinks that the advantages of group work are:

_____

_____

_____

Worksheet 3B

SECTION A: FOCUS ON TALK

4. USING THE GROUND RULES

Resources

Worksheets   *4A: Finding things*
                 4B: Taking turns to speak and listen

Aims

- To allow the groups to practise using their ground rules for talk in a structured context.
- To develop an understanding of personal morality.

Whole-class introduction

Explain the aims for Lesson 4 and ask the children to recall their ground rules. Tell the class that the groups are going to use the agreed ground rules to come to some decisions together.

Distribute *Worksheet 4B* and ask each group's most adept reader to be responsible for reading it out. The children must read through the worksheet together, before they hear the story. Next, the teacher (or a fluent reader) should read aloud the short story 'Finding things', from *Worksheet 4A: Finding things*.

Group work

Ask the groups to follow the instructions on *Worksheet 4B: Taking turns to speak and listen*. Groups can contribute their ideas (contained in their answers to the worksheet questions) to a class discussion about the story.

Whole-class plenary

Ask the children to reflect on the content of the session, and on the quality of their talk together:

Did your group use the ground rules for talk? Did you need to remind one another?
Do you think the rules helped you to answer the questions well?

Restate the lesson aims and discuss whether children feel that these have been achieved.

Extension work

- Each group could discuss and write an ending to the story.
- Groups could act out just their chosen 'ending', or the whole story including the ending.
- The class could discuss the citizenship issues raised by the story: friendship, stealing, ownership and making difficult choices.
- The structured format of Worksheet 4B could be used to:
   o discuss issues raised in other stories
   o undertake a joint problem-solving activity
   o organise work together at the computer
   o plan a science investigation.

FINDING THINGS

Class 5 were doing maths. Tanya liked the sort of maths she was doing. She had to use her ruler to measure the sides of a rectangle, then add up all four numbers to find out what the perimeter measured. She liked it because you could check if your adding up was right by measuring all the way round the rectangle. She was looking forward to moving on to bigger things, using the long tape measure—round the desk, round the carpet or round her friend Sam.

Tanya was using a ruler Sam had given her for her birthday. It wasn't very long, only 20 cm, but it was special because it had a picture of a tiger on it. Sam came back to the table and sat down. The work seemed to have a lot of red pen on it.

"Oh dear!" said Sam.

"Tanya, please bring me your work to mark," said Mrs Smith.

Isaac was drawing triangles. He didn't really like maths, but he was trying his hardest to draw the lines accurately. He was using a school ruler, and it had little notches all down each side. "Somebody's used this as a hammer!" thought Isaac. He carried on trying.

He had $2.40 on the desk in front of him, and he kept looking at the coins and rearranging them. This was Isaac's lunch money. Usually Mum could only give him $1.00 but today he was lucky and he was planning to buy a can of soft drink as a treat.

As Tanya went past him to the teacher's desk, Isaac saw something fall onto the floor. It was a ruler. It was quite short but it had perfectly straight edges. "Just what I need," thought Isaac. "I bet I can use that to do my triangles really well. Then Mum will be pleased when she comes to parents' evening." He picked up the ruler and drew a beautiful triangle with perfectly straight edges.

"Wow!" said Jo who was sitting next to him. "Cool ruler!" Then the bell went and everyone started packing up for recess.

"Out you go!" said Mrs Smith.

It was a warm day, so Sam and Tanya didn't stop to get their coats. They ran straight outside. The playground filled up with people. After ten minutes of running around, Sam and Tanya drifted back towards the door. The bell would ring soon. "Hey!" said Tanya. "Look… there on the windowsill." She ran over to the school building. Outside, on the windowsill, was some money.

Sam looked around. "Nobody about… I wonder who it belongs to?"

"I don't know," said Tanya. There was a $2 coin, a 20 cent coin and two 10 cent coins.

"Well, you found it, so it's yours," said Sam. "You can share it with me … we'll buy some chips on the way home."

"I don't know," said Tanya, again. The bell rang. She scooped up the money and put it into her pocket. She promised herself that she would think about it later.

SECTION A: FOCUS ON TALK

Worksheet 4A

The class divided into groups for computer work and art. Tanya and Sam went to art, where they were drawing pictures of a Greek temple. "I need my ruler," said Tanya to the teacher. "Can I go and get it?"

"Yes … don't be long."

Back in the classroom, the ruler was nowhere in sight. Tanya asked Mrs Smith and Mrs Smith asked the class: "Has anyone seen a ruler with a—what? Oh—a tiger on it?"

"Isaac was using one like that," said Paula, "before recess."

Isaac looked flustered. "Yes, but I put it back," he said. "I remember, because I picked up my dinner money and then I …" He stopped. "Oh no—I've left my dinner money outside. I took it out but I haven't got a pocket, and I put it down!" He ran out of the room as the teacher was saying, "Well, you'd better go and fetch it."

Tanya was horrified. How could she say that she had the money? Was it already too late to say so? She hadn't really meant to keep it, after all—had she? Would they believe her? But if Isaac had taken her ruler, it was fair that she kept the money, wasn't it? But what if she kept quiet and then Sam told everyone she had picked it up?

Isaac came back, nearly in tears. The money was gone. He would have to borrow enough to pay for his lunch, and somehow his Mum would have to find extra money tomorrow.

Jo thought of the ruler in her pencil case. She would throw it in the bushes on the way home. She couldn't use it in class now, because everyone would know it was Tanya's. And her Mum would ask where it had come from if she took it home.

"Tanya, what is wrong?" asked Mrs Smith.

Thinking Out Loud

Taking turns to speak and listen

Read these instructions aloud.

I am going to ask one person a question about the story. We will all listen to their ideas. I will ask why they think what they tell us, and we will all listen to their reasons.

Then that person will ask the next person, until we have all said what we think, and why we think it.

Next we can spend as long as we like talking together to decide on an answer to the question. We must try to agree on an answer.

I am going to put a tick in these boxes to show that everyone had a turn to answer a question at the start of our discussion.

In this activity we must:
- take turns to talk and listen
- make sure everybody has a chance to say something
- try to agree on a group answer to the question.

Right? Let's start with Question 1 …

Questions to discuss	Person 1	Person 2	Person 3	Person 4
1. What choices does Tanya have and what should she do?				
2. What choices does Jo have and what should she do?				
3. Is stealing money worse than stealing a ruler?				
4. Is it wrong to steal—why?				

SECTION A: FOCUS ON TALK

5. REASONING WITH GROUND RULES

Resources
Worksheets   *5A: Visitors to the dogs' home*
              5B: Dogs in the dogs' home

Aims
- To apply all the ground rules for talk to reasoning problems.
- To ask relevant questions.

Whole-class introduction
Explain the aims of the lesson to the children. Ask them to remember their ground rules for talk (which should be displayed on the wall of the classroom).

Introduce the activity by explaining that there are six stray dogs in the dogs' home. The staff of the dogs' home have made a list of them, describing their size, age, likes, dislikes and so on. (Provide *Worksheet 5B: Dogs in the dogs' home*, if you wish to explain this more fully.)

Explain that the dogs are available for adoption. On this particular day, five sets of people arrive at the dogs' home to look for a dog they can adopt and take home. We have some information about what sort of home they can give a stray dog. (Provide *Worksheet 5A: Visitors to the dogs' home* for further explanation.)

The task for the groups is to think about the dogs and the people, and to talk together to make decisions about which owners would suit which dog. For example, Jack the bloodhound is very big and that is a good reason for deciding that he would not suit Mrs Jenkins, who has a small home. The groups should be aware that they are practising using the ground rules and that their discussion is the most important outcome of the lesson. They must concentrate on:

- asking for and giving reasons for suggestions
- making sure everyone is heard
- considering all ideas before coming to a group decision.

The dog left over at the end of the day will unfortunately have to be 'put down'! This makes rational debate particularly crucial. (But for a reprieve, see 'Extension work'.)

Group work
Use the information to make decisions about which dog best matches which owner. The sheets can be cut up if this helps (scissors may be a distraction from contributing to successful group talk). Each group should give an example of which dog they have matched with which person, and support their decision with reasons.

Lesson 5

23

Whole-class plenary

Ask the children to reflect on the content of the session, and on the quality of their talk together:

How well did your group talk together to solve problems?
Did you find it was easy to agree on what to do?
Do you think the rules helped you to sort out the dogs and families successfully?

Extension work

- Dogs and owners could be stuck next to one another on a new sheet. Tell the groups that the 'condemned' dog may be rescued if they can talk together and decide on an ideal home/owners for the dog to go to. Set a time limit of five or ten minutes for this discussion. The group then explains their ideas and reasons to the class. A decision to reprieve the dog (or not!) is then made.
- Lesson 5A is optional, and can be used to extend the skills introduced in Lesson 5.

SECTION A: FOCUS ON TALK

VISITORS TO THE DOGS' HOME

The Weston Family
Mr John Weston and Mrs Sue Weston, Tim (aged 10) and Lisa (aged 8).
Their house is in a quiet street. It has a large garden.
Everyone is out all day at work or school but all are at home on weekends.
The park is 5 minutes away. Tim and Lisa like football and skateboarding.

Mrs Jenkins
Aged 75 and lives on her own. Small home with very small garden.
Family visitors: grandchildren Paul (aged 3) and Sarah (aged 1). Mrs Jenkins likes to walk to the newspaper shop to buy her lottery ticket.

The Khamran family
Mrs Suma and Mr Dijek Khamran, and Suki (aged 9).
Suki has a pony and two cats and now wants a dog. Her mother is not very keen on dogs.
Large house in the country with a large garden and paddocks all around.
All enjoy being out of doors.

The Carter Family
Mr Omar Carter, Keeley (aged 16) and Liam (aged 14).
They have a small house in town. Mr Carter works at home. Keeley and Liam love dogs.
Keeley wants to be a vet. Mr Carter would like a guard dog.

Lara Young
Lara (aged 30) has a ground floor flat with no garden. She is at home most days.
Her hobby is mountain walking and she would like a dog to take with her. Nephew Russell (aged 8) sometimes comes to stay in her flat.

Talk together to decide which dog will suit which family best. Remember to give reasons for your ideas.

Worksheet 5A

Thinking Out Loud   Copyright © 2006 Dawes, Mercer and Wegerif

THINKING OUT LOUD

DOGS IN THE DOGS' HOME

Jack
Bloodhound cross
Male
4 years
Size: Large. Friendly and affectionate
Eats: Large amounts of food
Guard dog: Yes
Likes: To sit by the fire and chew slippers
Dislikes: Cats

Jess
Mixed breed
Female
3 years
Size: Medium. Very lively.
Eats: Any kind of dog food
Guard dog: Yes
Likes: To chew and play with things
Dislikes: Staying inside

Scooter
Mixed breed
Male
6 months
Size: Small
Eats: Chips and chocolate. Must be put on a better diet
Guard dog: No
Likes: Going out to play and barking at birds and cats. Not really well trained
Dislikes: Doing as he's told

Max
Mixed breed
Male
5 years
Size: Medium. With a long coat needing a lot of brushing. Pulls a lot on the lead
Eats: Most things
Guard dog: Yes
Likes: Chasing a ball, cars
Dislikes: Being brushed and being shut in

Fifi
French poodle
Female
5 years
Size: Medium. Needs grooming and clipping
Eats: Chicken and ham
Guard dog: No
Likes: Children and other dogs
Dislikes: Rain and the vet

Cassie
Beagle
Female
11 years
Size: Small. Affectionate but shy
Eats: Milk and biscuits
Guard dog: No
Likes: To be patted and warm
Dislikes: Running, bikes and snow

Worksheet 5B

Copyright © 2006 Dawes, Mercer and Wegerif

SECTION A: FOCUS ON TALK

5A. RAINFOREST PHOTOGRAPHER

An optional lesson to follow Lesson 5

Resources
Sheets of 1 cm squared paper, pencils, rubbers, rulers, coloured crayons/felt tips

Aims
- To provide children with practice in using all the ground rules to reach decisions and accept joint responsibility.
- To provide practice in mathematical problem solving.

Whole-class introduction
This activity is a modified version of 'Battleships', in which children are paired to work with another pair (in groups of four). However, instead of sinking boats, the idea is to collect 'photographs' of a variety of animals within a given time. While there is a large degree of chance, problem-solving and reasoning skills are also necessary for guessing the positions of the animals.

Group work
Children are paired. Each pair draws two grids on squared paper. The grids have the letters A to O along the base, and the numbers 1 to 15 up the left-hand side (see example on page 29).

To prepare for play, each pair must first position their own animals on one grid. They must decide together which squares to use, and colour in the animals, using the following information:

- One giant anteater   8 squares
- Two jaguars   5 squares each
- Three nine-banded armadillos   4 squares each
- Four golden lion tamarins   4 squares each
- Five scarlet macaws   2 squares each
- Six tree frogs   1 square

The animals must be separated by empty boxes, but can meet diagonally. The groups of boxes that make up an animal must join along their edges, not diagonally. This completed grid must be kept hidden.

The idea is that the group members are photographers, and their aim is to 'photograph' all the other team's animals, by guessing which square they are in. Each pair starts with both a blank grid and their own completed grid. Toss a coin to decide which pair starts. The pair that

27

starts must talk together to decide a square using conventional grid referencing, for example, square G8. The opposing team have to reveal what is in that square (either a blank, or the name of the animal).

Every time the players guess a blank square, the opposing team must provide them with information about the whereabouts of one of their hidden animals. This is done by starting at the blank square, and counting how many squares away (counting up/down/across, but not diagonally) the nearest animal is. The team does not say in which direction the hidden animal is to be found.

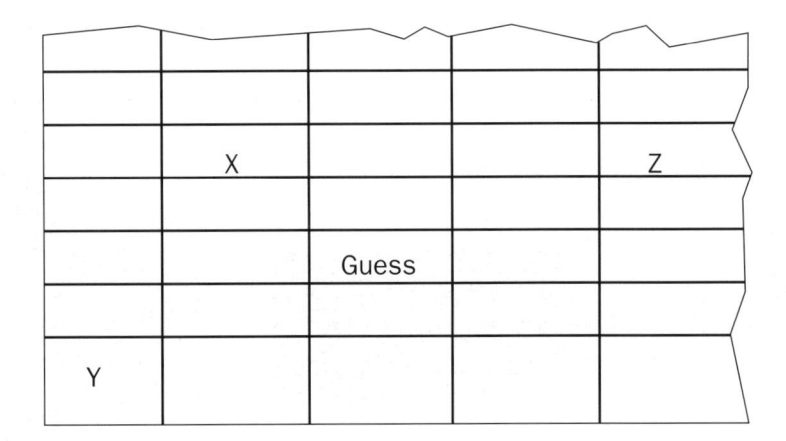

	X			Z
		Guess		
Y				

In this example, if X, Y and Z are tree frogs, the team's response would be: 'Blank but the nearest animal is 3 boxes away'. The aim is to 'photograph' all of the opponent's animals within the time limit. Pairs take turns to guess the contents of each other's 'rainforest'.

Whole-class plenary
Check how many animals have been photographed. Ask if the class can suggest variations on the rules of the game. Question the groups about the strategies that they used in order to find the animals. Restate the lesson aims and discuss whether children feel that these have been achieved.

SECTION A: FOCUS ON TALK

Extension work

- Suggest variations on this game, for example, Jungle safari using African animals; Sea-life food chain; Bird life; Australian wildlife; Space game (in which the items to be located are planets or constellations).
- Ask the class to devise their own versions.
- Children could also prepare grids to use with someone at home.

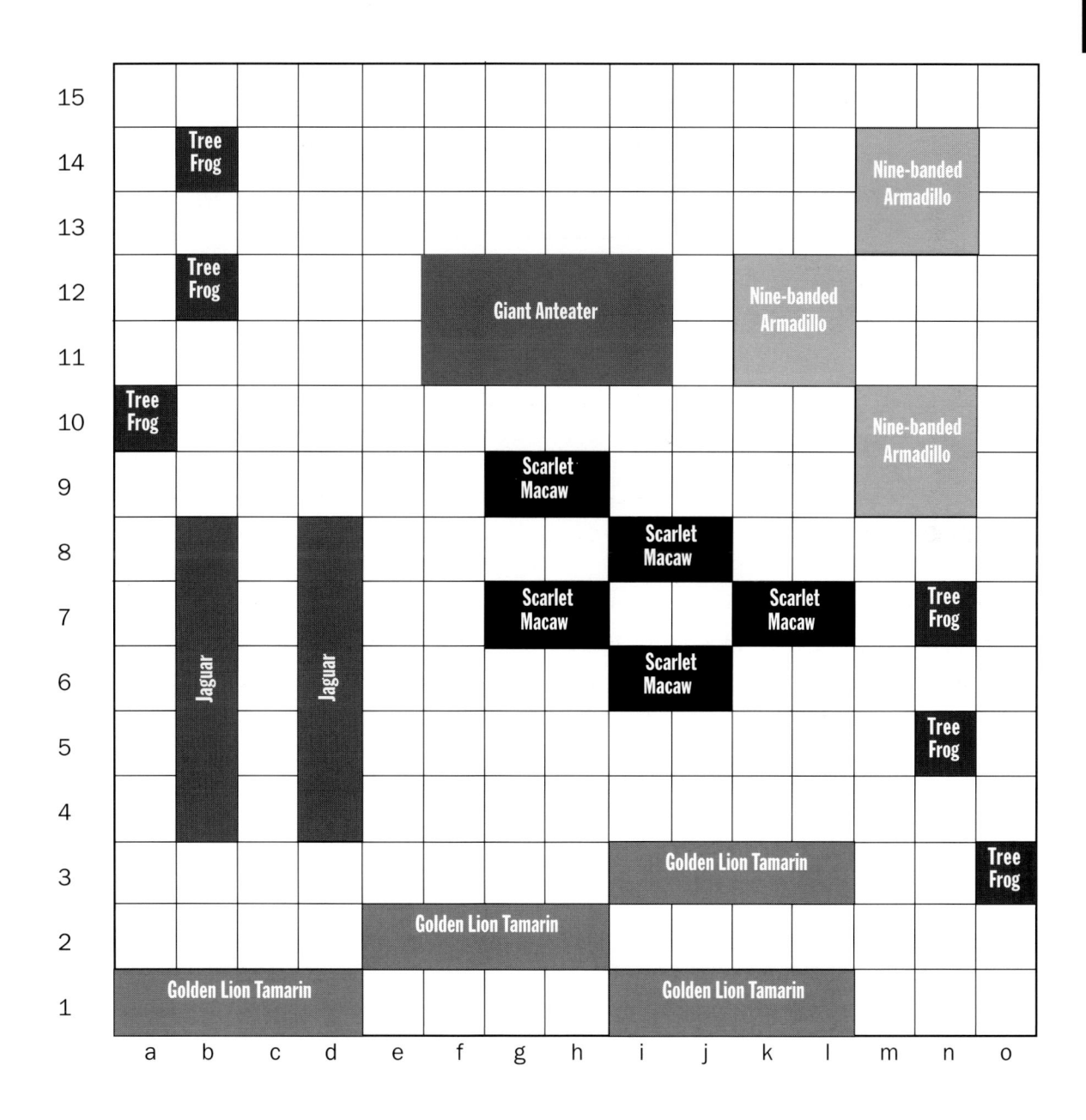

SECTION B
TALKING, THINKING AND LEARNING

THINKING OUT LOUD

6. PERSUASION

Resources
Worksheets   6A: Persuasive phrases
6B: Making a letter more persuasive

Aims
- To help children understand how language is used to persuade others.
- To teach the skills of persuasive talking and writing.

Whole-class introduction
Explain the aims for Lesson 6 to the children, and check that they understand the meaning of 'persuasion'. Briefly discuss some situations in which persuasion might be used, pointing out links between argument and agreement. Provide each group with a copy of *Worksheet 6A: Persuasive phrases*. Ask individuals to choose a phrase and use it in a sentence (spoken aloud). It might be necessary to provide a context for the persuasion, for example, to be taken swimming, shopping for a pizza or to a football match.

Group work

1. LETTER-WRITING

Provide *Worksheet 6B: Making a letter more persuasive*. Ask the groups to talk together to rewrite the letter and make it more persuasive. They could use some of the words and phrases from the previous activity.

2. ROLE-PLAY

Each group makes up a short scene in which one of them is a parent and the others are children. The scene should be based on one of the following scenarios in which the child wishes to:

- go to the disco
- stay up late to watch TV
- be given more pocket money
- have a friend to stay
- have hamburgers for tea
- be allowed to have a pet.

The groups must be prepared to present their scene to the class. The class discusses the effectiveness of the arguments and votes on what the parent should decide.

Whole-class plenary

Ask the children to reflect on the session content and on the quality of their talk together:

How well did your group work together?

Can you give an example of the way you shared your ideas through talk?

Extension work

- Children might be asked to discuss the ways that adults respond to persuasion. Discuss why adults might often end a discussion with phrases such as 'because I say so!' or 'when you get to my age …' Do children realise how much responsibility the adults have?
- Children could collect phrases or sayings about talk for illustration and display. Are they always true? These could be proverbs, or commonly-used phrases, such as: 'Actions speak louder than words', 'Don't do as I do, do as I say', 'Least said, soonest mended', and 'He is all talk'.
- Children could look at some of Aesop's fables, that present persuasive talkers, or talkers who brag, tell lies, or attempt to mislead. The moral purpose of the story may be obvious, but it is useful to consider the talk strategies employed by the characters.

Persuasive phrases

As a result …

To look at it in another way …

These are the facts …

I would like you to consider …

Because …

Do you think that …?

But …

On the other hand …

Perhaps we could discuss …?

Finally …

In my opinion …

In view of …

To sort this out we could …

Eventually …

Instead …

I can understand that …

Perhaps …

To resolve this matter …

Please …

I'd be glad if you'd think about …

Next time …

So …

My reason is …

Because …

Against that, it could be said …

To begin with …

The reason is …

Yet …

The best thing, I think, is to …

Maybe this time …

However …

We could decide together …

SECTION B: TALKING, THINKING AND LEARNING

MAKING A LETTER MORE PERSUASIVE

Worksheet 6B

95 Fountains Crescent
Mildura VIC 3500

Dear Aunty,

Thank you for offering to take me to the museum for my birthday but I don't want to go. Do we have to go? It's not fair. I don't even like museums. They are boring and full of old stuff. I want to go to the cinema. I need to see a film. You'll have to let me choose which one.

I will bring my friend along with me. I want to have popcorn and I am going to get a choc-top too. And not only that, it had better be the 9 o'clock session. Only little kids go early. You'd better take me to the cinema. Otherwise I will just be fed up and I will yawn a lot. If you don't like the cinema it is bad luck. You are just paying the money. It's my birthday and I can do what I like.

Best wishes,
From
Laura

THINKING OUT LOUD

7. KATE'S CHOICE

Lesson 7

Resources
Kate's choice software, available from www.thinkingtogether.org.uk

Worksheets   7A: Argument frame—Will Kate tell Robert's secret?
                 7B: Decision

Aims
- To apply all the ground rules to reasoning about social and moral issues.
- To use a computer program as a stimulus for thinking together.
- To deepen understanding of two citizenship issues (personal morality and the consequences of theft).

Whole-class introduction
Explain the aims of the lesson, stressing that the way the group talks together is an important focus. Raise and discuss the issue of keeping promises, asking the question: 'Is it ever right to break a promise?' Raise and discuss the issue of stealing from shops.

Group work

OPTION A: IF THERE ARE ENOUGH COMPUTERS FOR ALL TALK GROUPS

Ask the children to work through *Kate's choice* in their talk groups. Remind them of the ground rules for talk. Make sure that they have an agreed strategy for using the keyboard and mouse. Point out that the aim of the lesson is to do with talking and thinking so it is not important who uses the mouse and keyboard. Despite this, encourage children to swap after about ten minutes. The software will take about 15 minutes to work through. If groups finish quickly, ask them to try again taking a new route. Remind them to discuss problems together.

OPTION B: IF THERE ARE FEWER COMPUTERS THAN GROUPS

Give the whole-class introduction to the activity, and then arrange for some of the children to work on *Kate's choice* software in their groups while the other children are working on different group activities. When the whole class has had the opportunity to work on a computer, return to the plenary session.

Kate's choice
Kate has a friend called Robert who has a secret. He tells Kate the secret, on condition that she promises not to tell anyone else. It is his mother's birthday, and he has stolen a box of chocolates from a shop, to give to her. He decided to do this partly because his mother was ill. Kate has to decide whether to keep her promise or whether to tell and, if so, who she should tell. The children have to talk over the issues raised as Kate is put under pressure by various people. What choices are there for both Kate and Robert?

Whole-class plenary

Ask the children to reflect on the session content and on the quality of their talk together:

Can you share an example of someone giving a reason for their opinion?
What difference does it make to our decisions if we hear each other's reasons?

Extension work

Use Kate's choice as a stimulus for written argument either in the talk groups or for individuals using the 'argument frame' provided on *Worksheet 7A*.

USING ICT

The plan for Lesson 7 can be adapted and used with other software. *Thinking Out Loud* is an effective way of using software as a support for discussion. The aim of group discussion needs to be made explicit in the lesson aims. The plenary is crucial to ensure that children feel they have achieved the aims. Through this process, children become aware that their talk together at the computer is an important contribution to their learning. Successful learning is more likely to be achieved where the children do not rush through the lessons.

CHOOSING SOFTWARE TO ENCOURAGE TALK

Not all software will support thinking together. Sometimes the best software is the simplest. You can use this chart to analyse the potential of software for encouraging exploratory talk. Consider the software that you have used, or seen in use with children in the classroom, and tick the relevant boxes. Ticks in the 'yes' column indicate that the software design encourages and sustains discussion.

Questions	Yes	Partly	No
Is information which is useful for rational decision-making displayed on the screen?			
Are children offered choices that engage them in a continuing story or investigation?			
Are problems sufficiently complex?			
Do choices have important consequences?			
Are there multiple-choice options to encourage responses?			
Does the program encourage collaborative activity?			

Thinking Out Loud

Worksheet 7A

Will Kate tell Robert's secret?

Our decisions by (group names):

Reasons why she might:

Reasons why she might not:

Our decision is that Kate will choose to:

Our reasons for this decision are:

Other people might think this is wrong because:

We think Robert admitted to stealing the chocolates because:

We think he had some other choices which were:

What Robert's punishment might be and why:

Talking in a group was helpful because:

SECTION B: TALKING, THINKING AND LEARNING

DECISION

Our decision by (group names):

The problem is:

One point of view about this is:

We have talked together and decided to:

Because:

A particularly strong reason given by _____ was:

Useful information given by _____ was:

We think there may be further problems when:

Everyone has agreed to the decision. We know that things might not turn out as we expect, but we are sticking with it and sticking with each other!

Signed:

Worksheet 7B

Thinking Out Loud   Copyright © 2006 Dawes, Mercer and Wegerif

THINKING OUT LOUD

8. WHO PAYS?

Resources
Worksheets   8A: *Who pays?* (a short story)
  8B: *A discussion format*
  8C: *Drama cards* (to be photocopied and mounted separately on card)

Aims
- To use the ground rules for making joint decisions about social and moral dilemmas.
- To use discussion to increase children's awareness of the victims of crime.

Whole-class introduction
Explain the aims of the lesson to the children and ask them to remind each other of their ground rules for talk. Read, or ask a child to read, the short story on *Worksheet 8A*.

Remind the children that it is fine to disagree with another person's ideas, as long as they do so calmly and politely and can provide a reason for disagreeing. It is useful to stress that disagreeing with someone need not mean that you dislike that person. Reinforce the idea that a good discussion means that people do disagree, but listen to one another's reasons and are prepared to compromise.

Group work
Using *Worksheet 8B*, ask the groups of children to discuss the issues raised by the questions. Groups could then try the following activities:

1. Ask the groups to contribute to a whole-class discussion about the issues raised by the story.
2. Ask each group to make up a three-minute theatre play based on the drama cards provided on *Worksheet 8C*.

The children should read the drama cards together and decide how to present the story to the class. Only the simplest of props will be allowed and the script should not be written down. Each group presents its play with the rest of the class as audience.

Whole-class plenary
Ask the children to reflect on the content of the session, and on the quality of their talk together:
  Can you say how talking together helped your group to make decisions about the story?
  How did you manage to come to a group agreement?
  Can you give an example of how talk helped you to put your play together?

SECTION B: TALKING, THINKING AND LEARNING

Extension work
- Video or tape-record the children's plays.
- Use the set of plays as a basis for a whole-class discussion of the issues raised.
- Ask the children to write their own stories using the characters of Sam, Tanya, Henry, and any more they care to imagine. The story should tackle a problematic issue, for example, friendships, similarities and differences between people, telling the truth, respect, anger, appearances, rights and responsibilities. Stories do not have to resolve issues or have happy endings but should highlight potential problems caused by people's behaviour.
- Choose another story containing a moral dilemma and approach it in the same way. *Worksheet 8B* could be adapted for this purpose. Using this structure, the children could progress to independently organising their own discussions, using the ground rules for talk.

Who pays? A short story

The Mini-mart was a little shop on the corner of High Street and Clarence Road. Sam lived in Clarence Road and often went to the shop before school to buy chips, or a drink for her packed lunch.

Lots of other children went to the shop in the morning too. If the children had any pocket money, they would also go after school, to buy an ice-cream or sweets.

The shop was always full of children. Mr and Mrs Bell owned the shop. They kept it open very late in the evening and it was open all weekend too.

Sam didn't know how early they opened in the morning but it was much earlier than she ever got up. Mr and Mrs Bell's son Henry was in Sam's class at school and she knew that he often helped put things out on the shelves. It looked like fun.

Sam knocked on Tanya's door. "Ready?" They began walking to school.

Tanya was happy because the Book Fair was opening in school at lunchtime. She could choose a book to buy and she had enough money for the next book in her favourite animal series. "Are you going to buy a book, Sam?" she asked.

"Oh, I'd forgotten it started today," said Sam. "Well, maybe tomorrow. Look—I've only got $1.00 for my chips."

"Salt and vinegar as usual, I suppose," said Tanya.

There were lots of people in the shop. There were three girls from Year Seven and two boys from Year Six. A man in a suit was buying a box of chocolates and a lady with a small child in a pram was buying a newspaper.

Mr Bell was serving behind the till. It seemed very crowded in the little shop. Everyone was pushing past each other and tripping over the newspapers and the pram. Suddenly the shop emptied and Sam went to pay for her chips.

Mr Bell was looking worried and cross. "Look," he said to Sam and Tanya, "I'm fed up of you kids coming in here. I can't afford it any longer."

They looked at one another in surprise. What did he mean?

"Every morning and every afternoon this shop is full of kids," he said, waving his arms around. "Gangs—gangs of kids. And when you've gone, so have half of my boxes of lollies and whole packets of biscuits. Look! You can see now, four or five cans have gone, and no-one's paid for them."

They still couldn't think what to say. Mrs Bell came into the shop through the door at the back.

SECTION B: TALKING, THINKING AND LEARNING

"They've done it again. Taken a load of cans, and goodness knows what else," he said to her. "We just can't afford it any longer." He turned to Sam and took her money. "You kids, just taking things like that—and then Henry wants money to buy a book at school. How am I supposed to find money for books if people carry on stealing from us?"

Mrs Bell sat down on the chair behind the counter. She looked very sad. "What are we going to do?" she said. "It's hopeless. Henry works so hard for us when he'd really rather be out playing and yet we can't even give him the money for a book!"

Tanya was out of the door first. As Sam shut the door behind her, Tanya said, "Do you think they are poor, then? I always thought people who had shops were rich. They've got all that stuff, after all."

"Yes, and he said it was stealing, but it's shoplifting, isn't it?" said Sam. "Stealing from a shop isn't the same as stealing from a person, I reckon. And they are always open. They must make lots of money."

"I'm not so sure," said Tanya. "If people only buy packets of chips or newspapers or milk, you know, fairly cheap things, they would have to sell an awful lot to make any money for themselves."

"They made me feel as if it was my fault!" said Sam. "That's not fair."

They ran into the playground as the bell rang.

Worksheet 8A

Thinking Out Loud   Copyright © 2006 Dawes, Mercer and Wegerif

Thinking Out Loud

Who pays? A discussion format

Worksheet 8B

Instructions

Read the following instructions aloud in your group:

We are going to use the ground rules for talk to think together about the questions on this sheet. We will start by taking it in turns to say what we think and why, and I will put a tick in the boxes as that happens. Then we can discuss our ideas. Right? Let's start with Question 1 …

Questions for discussion:	Writer	1	2	3
Is shoplifting the same as stealing?				
What is the same about it? What is different?				
Is shoplifting wrong? Why?				
Would it be wrong for someone to 'shoplift' some food if they had no money and were very hungry?				
Which of the people in the shop was most likely to be a shoplifter? How can you tell?				
Sam thought it wasn't fair that Mr Bell was angry with her—do you agree?				
Does it matter more or less whether someone shoplifts from a small shop (like Mr and Mrs Bell's) or a big shop like Myer?				
How should shoplifters be punished?				

Copyright © 2006 Dawes, Mercer and Wegerif

SECTION B: TALKING, THINKING AND LEARNING

WHO PAYS? DRAMA CARDS

Scissors

Mr Smith watches as Luke goes into the stationery cupboard. Luke comes out with empty hands, but Mr Smith can see the handles of a pair of scissors sticking out of his pocket. He thinks Luke has stolen them. Luke has not been caught stealing before. But a lot of things have gone missing from the classroom recently and Mr Smith wants to make sure it stops.

What choices does Mr Smith have? What does he do? What does Luke say?

Brothers

Andy thinks that his older brother Paul has been stealing from the local shop. His friend Mark has told him that he saw Paul go along with a crowd of his friends and steal some lollies and drinks. He doesn't want to get Paul into trouble. On the other hand, Andy doesn't want Paul to be a thief.

What choices does Andy have? What should he do? What happens?

Treasure

You and a friend are playing near some bushes. Hidden under a bush you find a wallet carefully wrapped in a plastic bag. It has obviously been hidden there for some reason. Inside the wallet there is $60.00 in cash and a photograph but no name.

What choices do you have? What do you do? What happens?

Supermarket

You are out shopping in the supermarket. You notice that an elderly lady puts a tin of baked beans into her shopping bag and not into the trolley.

What choices do you have? What do you do? What happens?

Worksheet 8C

Thinking Out Loud   Copyright © 2006 Dawes, Mercer and Wegerif

Thinking Out Loud

Shopkeeper

Your friend has been caught stealing lollies from the shop. You have to go to the shop to get milk for your family. The shopkeeper follows you all round the shop. You ask why and he says he doesn't trust you. Then he asks you to leave.

Is this fair? What happens?

Ice-blocks

You and your sister go out to play. It is a hot day. You both get very thirsty but you are some way from home. Your sister tells you to wait outside the shop while she goes in to get some ice-blocks. You know that she doesn't have any money.

What do you say to her? What do you both do? What happens?

Windowsill

You and your friend are playing outside at lunchtime. You find $2.00 on the windowsill outside one of the classrooms. Your friend picks it up and says she will give it to the teacher. However, after school she offers you a chip from a packet that she has just bought. You realise that she kept the money.

What do you say? What does she do? What happens?

Bully

You meet the school bully outside the shop. He says he wants a Mars Bar and demands that you give him some money. You don't have any money. He says that unless you go in and steal a lolly for him, he will wait for you and beat you up on the way home.

Should you do as he says? What choices do you have? What happens?

SECTION B: TALKING, THINKING AND LEARNING

Worksheet 8C

Dares

You go out to play with your friends and you all decide to play 'dares'. The group dares someone to go into the shop and steal some chips. One of your friends manages to do it. You all share the chips. Then it's your turn. Your friends dare you to go and get some Smarties.

What choices do you have? What happens?

Apples

Your neighbour has an apple tree full of apples. She tells you that she is going to give them to your school for the Harvest Festival. But, that night, lots of the apples are stolen. Next day your friend offers you a bag of apples that have obviously come from the tree.

What choices do you have? What happens?

Watch

After PE, Tom's watch goes missing. Everyone looks but it is nowhere to be found. Tom is afraid his parents will be angry. That afternoon, you go round to play at your friend's house and you suddenly notice Tom's watch in your friend's bedroom.

What do you say? What does your friend say? What happens?

Rewards

It is near the end of term and the teacher has brought in a bag of lollies to give to students who have earned a reward. At break, you go back to collect something from the classroom and you notice that the bag is open on the desk. You would love a lolly and think it would be all right if you took one for your friend too. Then you think again.

What do you decide to do? Why? What would someone else do?

Thinking Out Loud   Copyright © 2006 Dawes, Mercer and Wegerif

THINKING OUT LOUD

9. WATER VOLES

Resources
The following resources are for the 'Water vole' board game:

Information sheets *9A: About the water vole*
9B: How to make the water vole game (for the teacher)

Game sheets *9A: Water vole game: people information*
9B: Water vole game: labels
9C: Water vole game: chance cards
9D: Water vole game: rules
9E: Water vole colony cards (set)
9F: 'Water vole year' (board game)

Before the lesson, please follow the instructions on *Information sheet 9B*.

Aims
- To encourage children's critical questioning and reasoning.
- To give children more practice in making joint decisions and presenting ideas as a group.
- To deepen awareness of issues in ecology.

Whole-class introduction
Explain the aims of the lesson and ensure that the children recall the importance of using the ground rules for talk in their discussions. Use *Information sheet 9A* to give a brief description of the plight of water voles as they move towards extinction in England. Then explain the object and rules for the board game, as follows:

RULES

The object of the game is to go through a year along the river, finding out what factors affect the water vole colonies. Colonies can be lost or gained. Players shake a die and move along the 'river'. If they land on a chance square, they take a chance card. Some of the cards direct the players to listen to the opinions of various people who wish to alter the riverbank. One player should read out each opinion.

The group then discusses the opinion (using their ground rules for talk) and decides whether or not to approve the change proposed. When all players have landed on the last square, the group should assess the river to see how many water vole colonies have survived.

See *Game sheet 9D* for a detailed list of the rules.

SECTION B: TALKING, THINKING AND LEARNING

Group work
Ask the children to work through the board game in their talk groups. Compare results of the board game, as a class. Change groups—new groups need not be the usual talk groups—and start again with the game. The ground rules for talk should still apply. To make things more difficult (or realistic) groups could start from the position they were in at the end of the previous 'year'. Finally, ask the children to evaluate the quality of their discussions.

Whole-class plenary
Ask the children to reflect on the content of the session, and on the quality of their talk together:

How well did your group work together?
Can you give an example of changing your mind because you heard a good reason?

Extension work
Find out more about water voles from as many sources as possible—books, CD-ROMs, conservation groups, the Internet.

Look at a different conservation issue involving loss of species through habitat destruction, for example:

- mahogany trees in the Amazon rainforest
- mountain gorillas in Rwanda
- whales in the waters around Japan
- cod in the North Atlantic
- polar bears in the Arctic Circle
- kiwi in New Zealand
- platypuses in Australia
- tigers in Siberia
- snow leopards in Tibet.

Consider the kinds of actions by local people that cause habitat destruction, in terms of the lives of the local people. What issues arise? What are the similarities with the problems for water voles?

THINKING OUT LOUD

Info sheet 9A

ABOUT THE WATER VOLE

The water vole was immortalised as 'Ratty' by Kenneth Grahame in *The Wind in the Willows*, published in 1908. Water voles found it increasingly difficult to survive as their riverside environment changed throughout the last century. They are now the most endangered British mammals. The board game demonstrates some of the uses people have found for river banks, and asks the children to discuss their opinions on whether the needs of water voles or the requirements of people should be given priority.

Water voles prefer slow-moving water and river banks that are rich in vegetation. They excavate burrows in the banks and line them with shredded rushes or reeds. They are herbivorous, feeding on grasses, rushes and sedges from the banks, and fruits and roots in autumn and winter. Water voles live in colonies along the banks and breeding begins in March or April. In April or May, two to six young are born. At first they are helpless—blind, hairless and toothless—but by ten days old they have become miniature versions of the adults and at 28 days they are weaned.

The water vole has a wide range of traditional predators, including foxes, otters, stoats, weasels, rats, owls, herons, raptors and large fish. Domestic cats can also cause extinction of local colonies. A new problem is the rising number of American mink, either escaped, or released from fur farms. Studies have shown that water vole populations within the territories of breeding female mink can be decimated within a year. Loss of habitat is another cause of population reduction. Some estimates put the population of water voles as low as 200,000 (that is 3,000 colonies). These numbers may sound large but the water vole is at the bottom of the food chain: there are, for example, 37 million rabbits in Britain, 31 million moles, and 75 million field voles. The water vole used to be common, but is now scarce.

Further information on water voles
- Strachan, R 1997 *Water Voles*, Whittet Books Ltd., London.
- Water Vole Steering Group: Environment Agency, Kings Meadow House, Kings Meadow Rd, Reading RG1 8DQ.
- The British Waterways Environmental and Scientific Services: Llanthony Warehouse, Gloucester Docks, Gloucester GL1 2BJ.
- BBOWT (Berks, Bucks & Oxon Wildlife Trust) 1 Armstrong Road, Littlemore, Oxford, OX4 4XT

Web sites
www.bbc.co.uk/nature/wildfacts/factfiles/268.shtml
www.arkive.org/species/ARK/mammals/Arvicola_terrestris

SECTION B: TALKING, THINKING AND LEARNING

HOW TO MAKE THE WATER VOLE GAME

1. Each group should have a *Water vole year* board game (*Game sheet 9F*) preferably A3 size, which they can colour and laminate, if necessary.

2. Each group should have a copy of *Game sheet 9A: people information*. This should be cut up into nine separate identities and glued on to card, with the appropriate label (from *Game sheet 9B*) stuck on to the reverse side of the card. These are then placed face down next to the board.

3. The chance cards (*Game sheet 9C*) should be cut up, glued on to card, and placed face down on the board.

4. The water vole colonies (on *Game sheet 9E*) should also be backed with card. Place eight of the colony cards on the board, and the rest beside the board.

5. Each child has a counter, to be placed at the beginning.

6. Before starting, the groups should read the instructions (*Game sheet 9D*) and check that they understand how to play the game. They should also know what the aims of the game are. They should not read through the people information or chance cards.

Info sheet 9B

THINKING OUT LOUD

WATER VOLE GAME: PEOPLE INFORMATION

Game sheet 9A

Animal rights activist

I love animals. I think they have the right to be wild and free. 'Activist' means I take action—and I take action to help animals. Near here there is a mink farm. Mink are little furry creatures like cats, but fiercer, and they can swim. They are from America. The mink farmer keeps them in tiny metal cages. Then when they are big enough, he kills them, skins them and sells their fur to make coats. It is very cruel. It shouldn't be allowed. The mink are suffering. I am going to go and let them all out of their cages so that they can be free. That will teach the mink farmer a lesson.

I know that mink eat lots of water voles. But the water voles can look after themselves. They can breed to replace the ones that get eaten. It is more important to let those poor creatures out of their cages than it is to worry about a few water voles. There are plenty more of them. Mink eat rats too, so they are useful really. Helping water voles survive isn't my problem at the moment—think of the mink.

I am going to free as many mink as I can—why not?

Fisherman

I love animals. I love fish and that's why I like to catch them. I don't think water voles matter very much except that they are good food for the pike. I want to be able to sit nearer the water so I want the edge of the bank flattened. The water voles have dug out the bank and made it crumbly so I think we should get it repaired and have proper concrete platforms put along here; then people can use it again.

My hobby costs me a lot of money. I pay for this river to be kept clean and tidy so that I can fish in it. Because I pay money, I am good for the environment—the Environment Agency makes sure the water pollution levels stay low, so that there are always fish. I have the right to a good place to fish. The water voles can go and live somewhere else.

I am going to campaign for concrete platforms to be put along the bank—why not?

SECTION B: TALKING, THINKING AND LEARNING

Game sheet 9A

Farmer

I love animals. I know all about them—which most people don't. I also know that people need to eat and I have to grow their food. It doesn't come from nowhere to the supermarket, you know! Things have been difficult recently, with the bad weather. Now I am going to plough up the field next to the river, because I have to. When I do this, I will get some money from the government so I will be able to buy a new tractor and grow more food.

I will be able to get some good seed for next year and grow some sugar beet in the field. It will grow well there. There is plenty more river for water voles. It is only one field, or maybe two, and I need the money. Look—if I grow the sugar beet it can be turned into sugar for sweets—you wouldn't like to go without those, would you? Where are you going to get food from, if I don't grow it?

I am going to plough up the field by the river—why not?

Dog owner

I love animals. I've got one—this dog. You might call those things water voles, but they look like rats to me. I get my dog to chase them. It's fun, and doesn't do any harm. It doesn't hurt them you know. They don't feel things like we do. And they are vermin: they are just like rats and can spread disease.

Me and my dog are doing you a favour by catching a few. Anyway my dog is an animal too and he needs the exercise. It's good for a dog to run after other things. It's only natural. I've always trained my dogs to go after rats and rabbits. Otherwise the countryside would be overrun by them like in Australia. There would be too many and the grass would die. I can do what I like anyway.

I am going to get my dog to chase them—why not?

Thinking Out Loud   Copyright © 2006 Dawes, Mercer and Wegerif

THINKING OUT LOUD

Game sheet 9A

Land developer
I love animals. My job is to build homes for people and their pets. I have to find empty places to build new homes. People have to live in houses, and there aren't enough of them. How would you like it if you were homeless? I turn empty spaces into wonderful new housing estates with homes for people who need them. I don't think a few holes for water voles should stand in the way of homeless people getting somewhere to live, do you? And by the river here, the houses will have a lovely view.

We can tidy up the bank and have a nice path, so people can walk without getting muddy. The water voles really ought to be living somewhere else, I think. They could keep them safe in a zoo or take them to another river. People need houses. They don't need water voles.

I am going to build a housing estate—why not?

Factory owner
I love animals. I have some terrific guard dogs at my factory. My factory is just up the river from here. It has been there a long time. We take water from the river to cool the machinery, then we put it back in. I have spent a lot of money on cutting down the pollution we put into the water. We are doing our best. There might be the odd leak of poisonous chemicals sometimes but it is always an accident. If it kills off the fish and water voles, it can't be helped. They always come back, don't they?

The thing is, I employ 250 people. I pay their wages so they can feed their kids and buy them new trainers, trips to the cinema and birthday presents. I can't help it if there are accidents at the factory sometimes. My machines are getting a bit old and I could spend more money on making sure they don't poison the river. But if I do, I will have to cut people's wages.

I am going to keep on using the river like I always have—why not?

SECTION B: TALKING, THINKING AND LEARNING

Boat owner

I love animals. My cat comes with me on the boat. It is a canal boat. We want to use this bit of river to link one canal with another. It just needs the sides straightening. It would only take a week or so with a JCB digger and it would be done. Very neat and tidy. Then lots of boats could come up and down here.

People like boat trips, and it helps stop cars polluting the air if people use boats. It is only a small stretch of river—there is plenty more for the water voles in other places. The boats will make money so the Environment Agency can keep the water quality good, too. It will be very good for the river. Just think, you could go on a boat trip down here—wouldn't that be fun?

I am going to straighten out the banks of the river—why not?

Park keeper

I love animals. I have cages with rabbits in the park. The park is just along the river and we have swans and ducks and moorhens. We make sure that they are looked after. If we made the riverbank part of the park, we could have more swans and ducks and moorhens. We would need to tidy it up though. Those willow trees are leaning over the water in a way that is dangerous. What if one of them fell on someone?

We could tidy up the bushes so that there would be a better view. Then people could walk here more easily. If we had a park here, they would never be able to build houses on it. People could come here and play football, or ride bikes, or whatever they liked. There is plenty of wildlife out in the countryside. In town, we need to use the land for people.

I am going to get my whipper snipper and sort out that riverbank—why not?

Thinking Out Loud   Copyright © 2006 Dawes, Mercer and Wegerif

THINKING OUT LOUD

Game sheet 9A

Most people

We love animals. We have pets and bird feeders in the yard. But water voles are like rats, and rats are dirty creatures that spread disease. We have never seen a water vole, so they can't be that important. You can live without water voles. It is more important to have good homes, plenty to eat, and good facilities like parks. Who says that water voles are endangered? It's probably not true. They are probably just saying it to get some money from us. It might be nice to have them in the river, but there are minks here now and they are just as interesting.

Anyway if water voles are nearly extinct, it's too late to worry about it. There are probably millions of them in Norway or somewhere. It's the Amazon rainforest we should be worrying about. We have stopped buying furniture made from rainforest timber, so we are doing our bit. Did you say that there are practically no voles left here?

That's a shame, but I'm going to carry on doing nothing about it—why not?

SECTION B: TALKING, THINKING AND LEARNING

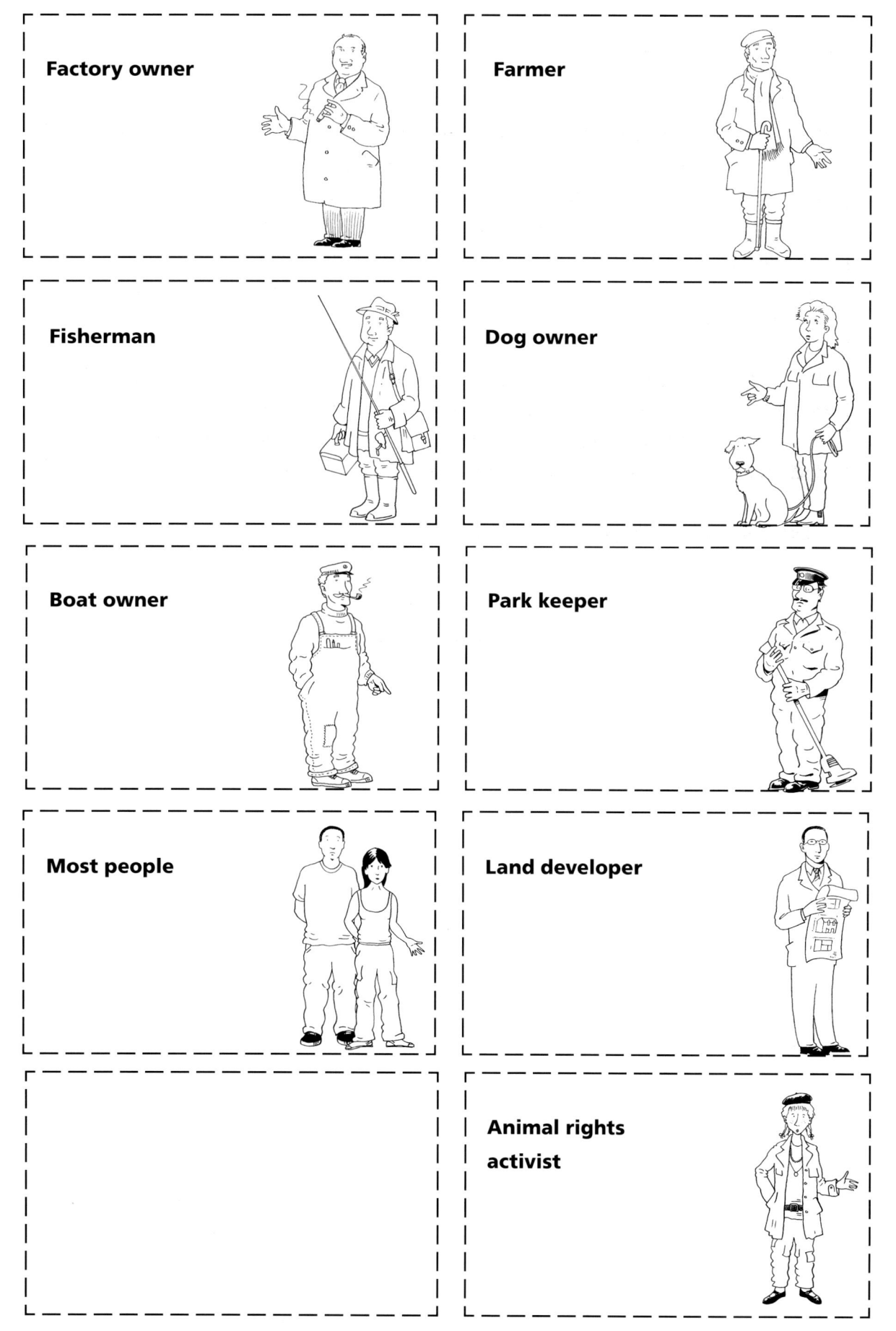

WATER VOLE GAME: LABELS

Factory owner	Farmer
Fisherman	Dog owner
Boat owner	Park keeper
Most people	Land developer
	Animal rights activist

Game sheet 9B

Thinking Out Loud

Water vole game: chance cards

School children measure water pollution: water vole family moves in!	**FLOOD!** Lose a water vole family.
School children do a water vole survey: water vole family moves in!	**MINK!** Eats a water vole family.
School children do a litter collection: water vole family moves in.	**PIKE!** Eats a water vole family.
School children write to the Environment Agency: water vole family moves in.	**FOX!** Eats a water vole family.
School children learn about water voles: water vole family moves in.	**HERON!** Eats a water vole family.

Game sheet 9C

SECTION B: TALKING, THINKING AND LEARNING

WEASEL! Eats a water vole family.	Let's hear what the **FISHERMAN** has to say.
Let's hear what the **ANIMAL RIGHTS ACTIVIST** has to say.	Let's hear what the **DOG OWNER** has to say.
Let's hear what the **FARMER** has to say.	Let's hear what the **FACTORY OWNER** has to say.
Let's hear what the **LAND DEVELOPER** has to say.	Let's hear what the **BOAT OWNER** has to say.
Let's hear what the **PARK KEEPER** has to say.	Let's hear what **MOST PEOPLE** have to say.

WATER VOLE GAME: RULES

1. The game is for two to four players.

2. The aim of the game is to discuss some of the things that make it easier or harder for water voles to survive.

3. Set out the board as follows:

   - Put the chance cards on the 'chance cards' box.
   - Put the people information cards (face down) to one side.
   - Put one counter for each player at the beginning of the game.
   - Put eight water vole colony cards out along the riverbank.

4. Decide who goes first: shake the dice and move along the board. When you get to a chance square, take a card from the board and follow the instructions. (The group can decide who reads out the people information cards.)

Remember to talk about the ideas.

If the group decides to agree with the people information card, a water vole colony card is removed from the board. If the group disagrees with the people card, the colonies stay as they are.

5. When everyone has landed on 'end', count up the colony cards:

   - more than eight colonies—the water voles will survive for another year;
   - four to seven colonies—the water voles may survive, but will need good luck and help;
   - less than four colonies—the water voles are dangerously close to vanishing from this river;
   - less than two colonies—the water voles will become extinct here.

SECTION B: TALKING, THINKING AND LEARNING

WATER VOLE COLONY CARDS

Game sheet 9E

Thinking Out Loud   Copyright © 2006 Dawes, Mercer and Wegerif

61

Game sheet 9F

THINKING OUT LOUD

WATER VOLE YEAR

BEGIN MARCH 21ST

SPRING

2

3

APRIL 21ST

5

CHANCE

MAY 21ST

SUMMER

JUNE 21ST

8

7

11

10

12

JULY 21ST

14

15

16

AUGUST 21ST

If you land on a ✻ square, take a chance and talk about it.

62   Copyright © 2006 Dawes, Mercer and Wegerif

SECTION B: TALKING, THINKING AND LEARNING

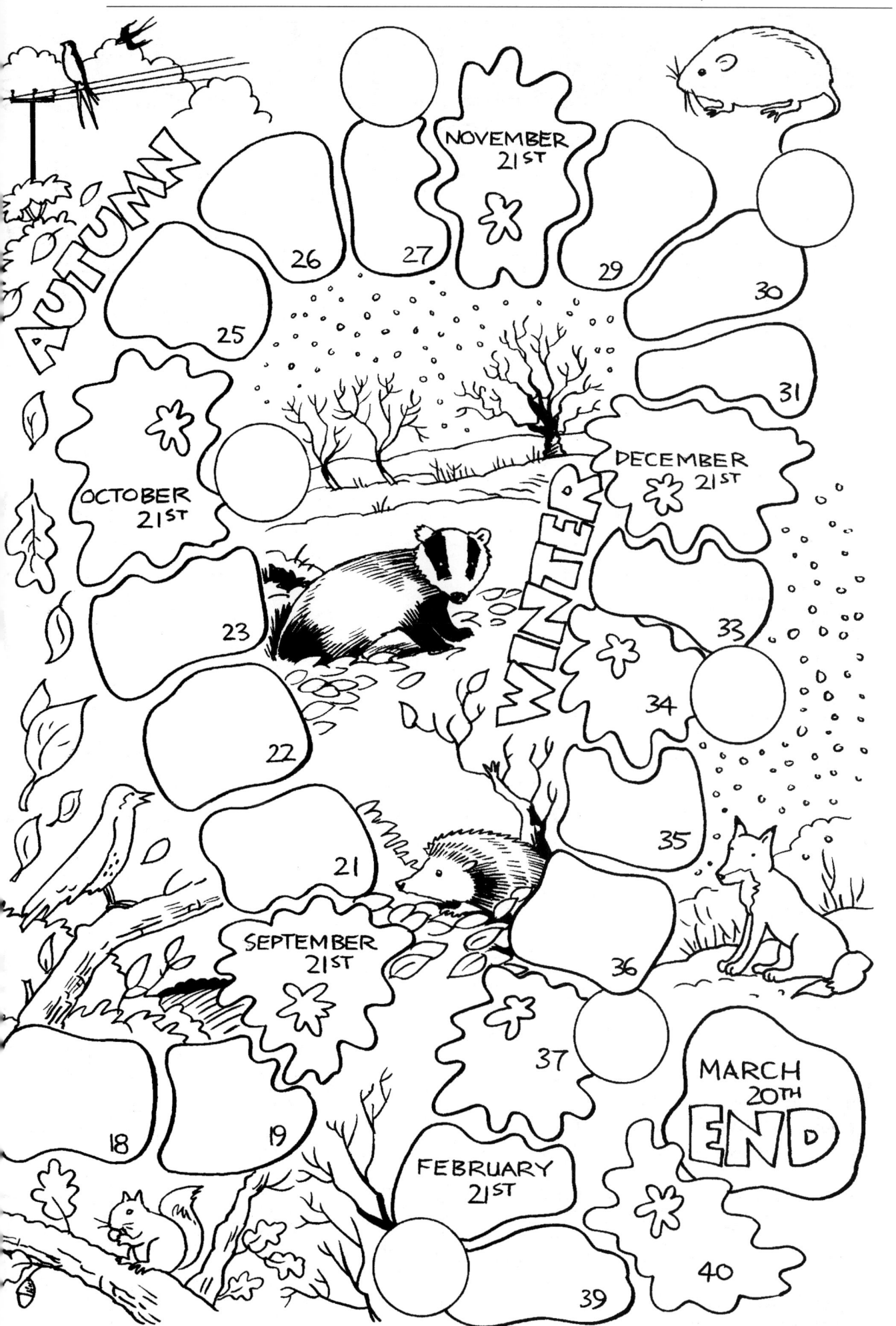

Game sheet 9F

AUTUMN

NOVEMBER 21ST

26 27 29 30

25

31

OCTOBER 21ST

DECEMBER 21ST

23

WINTER

33

34

22

35

21

36

SEPTEMBER 21ST

37

MARCH 20TH END

18 19

FEBRUARY 21ST

39 40

Thinking Out Loud   Copyright © 2006 Dawes, Mercer and Wegerif

63

THINKING OUT LOUD

10. TOWN PLAN

Resources
Worksheets   *10A: Town plan*
10B: Facilities
10C: Information items

Aims
- To develop children's ability to provide clear instructions and act upon them.
- To encourage joint decision-making, using all the ground rules for talk.
- To promote awareness of planning and environmental issues.

Whole-class introduction
Using the following information, explain the lesson aims and the town planning activity to the children. The task for each group is to plan the best possible new town. To do this, each group should discuss how they could arrange the new facilities on the town plan. Some of the facilities are:

- swimming pool
- toilets
- petrol station
- school
- church
- factory.

The group must consider and decide where, in the town, they think each facility should be. Remind children of the ground rules for talk, and to try to come to a group decision, giving reasons for all their ideas. Provide a copy of *Worksheets 10A* and *10B* for each group.

Worksheet 10C: Information items gives directions and reasons for the positioning of six of the facilities (those listed above). Cut up the sheet into separate items and give each talk group in the class one item (or more if there are less than six groups).

Group work
When any group requires information about another facility, it should send one member to visit the group with the appropriate information. Members of the 'information-holding' group should take it in turns to read to the 'information-seeking' visitors. The visitor is not allowed to read the information or write it down, but must listen and remember it to repeat to their own group. Each member of the group must carry out this task in turn, as the need arises.

Set up a whole-class discussion about the position of facilities in the new town, giving reasons for their ideas.

SECTION B: TALKING, THINKING AND LEARNING

Whole-class plenary

Ask the children to reflect on the content of the session, and on the quality of their talk together:

Can you give an example of people in your group thinking of different ideas?
What did you have to do to help you make a group decision?
Do you think your group talked well together? Why?

Extension work

- Display the town plans, with written reasons for the choice of layout.
- Try to think of reasons why your local town, village or city is laid out as it is.

THINKING OUT LOUD

TOWN PLAN

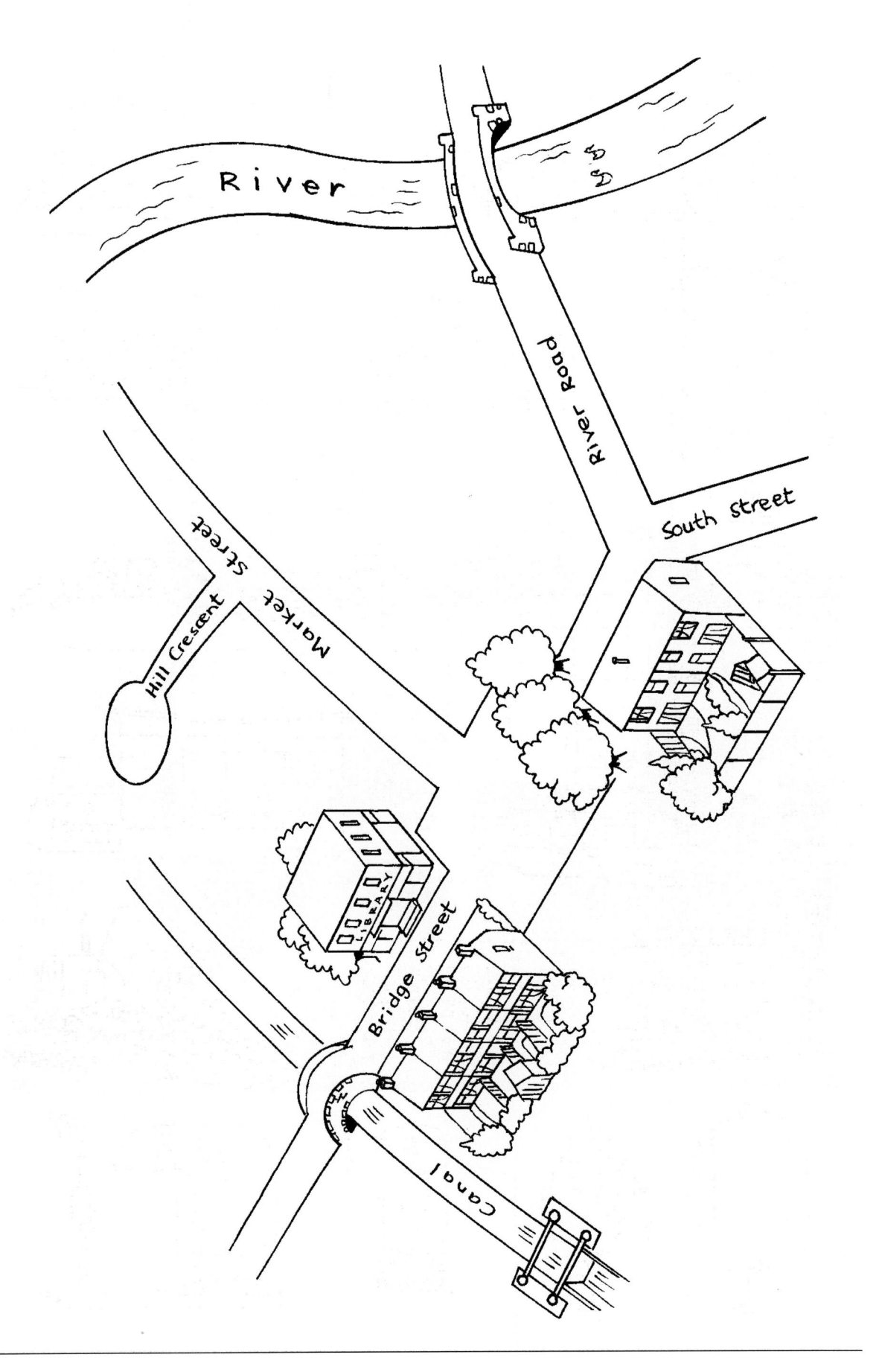

SECTION B: TALKING, THINKING AND LEARNING

FACILITIES

Worksheet 10B

Thinking Out Loud   Copyright © 2006 Dawes, Mercer and Wegerif   67

THINKING OUT LOUD

INFORMATION ITEMS

Swimming pool

The swimming pool must be near to the school, because the children need to go for lessons, and the school does not have a minibus. It should also be quite near the car park, because people don't like walking too far to their cars when they are tired.

Toilets

These must be near the park so that people can find them easily, when they are out. They must also be near the shops for the same reason.

Petrol station

This must not be too near the houses as it could be a fire risk.

School

This must not be too near the petrol station which could be a fire risk. It should also be away from the rubbish tip, which would be bad for children's health.

Church

This must be near the centre of the town so it is within walking distance for people who want to go there.

Factory

This must not be near the houses or school, because it is noisy. It should be near the car park so that people can park there to go to work.

11. A FAIR TEST

Resources
Six or more 'kitchen cupboard' chemicals to display, e.g. white, cube or brown sugar; flour; custard powder; Epsom salts; cornflour; oat bran; ground rice; rock or table salt; nutmeg; corn oil; gravy powder or granules and so on
Worksheet 11: Talking about an investigation

Aims
- To give children practice in making joint decisions and presenting ideas as a group.
- To apply the ground rules to define a hypothesis and plan a 'fair test' for investigation.

Whole-class introduction
Explain the lesson aims, then show the children the different 'chemicals'. Make it clear that they might be edible in the kitchen but in science lessons all chemicals are regarded as poisonous and must not be put in or near the mouth. Check that the children understand what is meant by the words *dissolve* and *solution*. Ask them to explain these terms in their own words. Then, describe the following science problem to the class:

KITCHEN CHEMICALS: AN INVESTIGATION ABOUT DISSOLVING

It was raining and Isaac and Simon had nothing to do. They had to stay in. They decided they would act out being scientists and turn the kitchen into a science laboratory.

"We need some chemicals to mix," said Isaac.

"There are lots of things in the cupboard," said Simon. "Everything is a chemical really! We should do an experiment."

"OK, an investigation. Let's find out which of these chemicals dissolves in water," said Isaac, pouring sugar into a cup full of water.

"Hang on!" said Simon. "If we really want to know, we have to do a fair test to find out."

The group's task is to design a fair test investigation to find out which of the chemicals will dissolve in water.

Give each group a copy of *Worksheet 11* and stress the need to use the ground rules for talk in this planning activity.

Group work
Using *Worksheet 11*, each group must write down their hypothesis stating which chemicals will dissolve, with reasons, and which will not, with reasons, and plan an investigation to test their hypothesis.

Each group pairs up with another group and shows what they have decided to do. Then, in turns, each group should state and justify their hypothesis and make clear how they will ensure that they conduct a fair test. Members of the other group can ask questions about this. In a whole-class discussion, individuals should give an account of their group's ideas and hypothesis.

Whole-class plenary
Ask the children to reflect on the content of the session, and on the quality of their talk together:
> *Can you provide an example of a prediction and a reason for it?*
> *Did you find it difficult to agree on a prediction?*
> *What did you do to end up in agreement?*

Extension work
- Let the groups carry out the investigation. Each group should decide on how best to display its results.
- Review the importance of the use of the ground rules in this work.
- Ask individual students to plan a similar investigation, for example, to see if substances dissolve at different rates in warm water or to decide which ice cube (of four different shapes) will melt fastest when dropped in water. This time, allow no conferring, discussion of ideas or sharing of information. Once the plans are complete, organise a class discussion to decide which is the most effective way to plan an investigation, either in groups using the ground rules, or alone.
- *Worksheet 11* can be adapted to provide a document which will support discussion at the planning stage of any science investigation.

SECTION B: TALKING, THINKING AND LEARNING

TALKING ABOUT AN INVESTIGATION

Step 1

Discuss the following: What shall we actually do? Can we draw a diagram to show this? What equipment shall we use?

Step 2

Discuss the following: To make it a fair test, what one thing will we change each time? What things will we make sure stay the same?

Step 3

Discuss the following: How will we record our results?

Step 4

Discuss the following: Before we do the investigation, we have to predict which chemicals will dissolve. (That is, we have to say what we think and give a reason for it.) Complete the following.

Our prediction is that these chemicals will dissolve because:

_____

_____

Our prediction is that these chemicals will not dissolve because:

_____

_____

These are our group's ideas. Signed:

_____

Worksheet 11

Thinking Out Loud   Copyright © 2006 Dawes, Mercer and Wegerif

THINKING OUT LOUD

12. Non-fiction

Lesson 12

Resources
Dictionaries and thesaurus
Worksheets   *12A: Goosebumps*
                       12B: Friction
                       12C: Questioning texts

Aims
- To encourage children to use the ground rules for talk to discuss a written text.
- To develop children's ability to read for meaning.
- To deepen understanding of friction as a scientific concept.

Whole-class introduction
Explain the aims of the lesson to the children and ask them to remember the ground rules for talk. Remind the children that their talk together is of paramount importance and that in this lesson they will use their spoken language to improve their reading. Provide each group with a copy of *Worksheet 12A* or display the text using an overhead projector/whiteboard. Ask fluent readers to read the text out loud to the class. Explain that the class will ask questions about the text so that everyone understands its meaning. Check that the children understand what a paragraph is. Guide them towards deciding together on the following:

- any words that must be clarified by looking in a dictionary or by talking to one another
- three 'keywords' for each paragraph
- a summary of what each paragraph is about
- two questions that each paragraph would answer
- a new title for the text.

Group work
Use *Worksheet 12B: Friction*. Ask the groups to talk together to establish meaning from the text, as in the whole-class work. *Worksheet 12C* provides a structure for the group discussion. Ask groups to contribute their agreed ideas to a class discussion.

Whole-class plenary
Ask the children to reflect on the session content and on the quality of their talk together:
Did the discussion with your group help you to understand the writing?
Did you remember to use the ground rules for talk? Can you give an example?

Extension work
- Ask each group to compile a pamphlet or poster on the topic of 'friction' using what they have learnt, as well as other sources.
- The structure of *Worksheet 12C* can be adapted to support group discussion about non-fiction texts.

SECTION B: TALKING, THINKING AND LEARNING

GOOSEBUMPS

Why do I get goosebumps when I'm cold?

Goosebumps is your skin trying to keep you warm! You belong to a group of animals called mammals. All mammals can feed their babies with milk. Mammals don't have feathers or scales—they have skin with hair or fur. Hair keeps you warm. It does this by trapping a warm layer of air next to the skin. When any furry mammal gets cold, its hair 'stands on end'. That makes the hair hold even more air, which keeps the warmth in.

You wear clothes to keep you warm. But your skin and hair still work like any other mammal. The hair you do have, even though there isn't much of it, can 'stand on end' to hold air and to help keep you warm. The 'bumps' of goosebumps are where you can see this happening, at the roots of the hair on your skin.

You get goosebumps when you are scared, too. This time your hair stands on end to make it stick out more, and make you look bigger and fiercer. Have you ever noticed that cats and dogs do this when they are scared? They get goosebumps too!

Worksheet 12A

Thinking Out Loud   Copyright © 2006 Dawes, Mercer and Wegerif

THINKING OUT LOUD

FRICTION

1. Isaac Newton was a brilliant scientist. He thought about the way things seemed to work in the world around him and then tested his ideas to see if they were right. He was very interested in the way light works, in maths and in the way things move. He tried to find out what makes things move and stop. He found out that things started moving if there was a force pushing or pulling them, or turning them round. Newton made a list of rules or laws which describe the way things move in our universe. Another word for movement is 'motion'. We call his rules *Newton's Laws of Motion*.

2. This is one of *Newton's Laws of Motion*: Every moving thing in the universe carries on moving just as it is, unless a force acts on it to stop it or to change its direction. But we seem to see moving things stop all by themselves. If we kick a ball along the ground it will soon slow down and stop moving. The ball started moving because it was kicked. A kick is a pushing force. The force of the kick makes the ball move. But what stops it moving? It just seems to stop when it has run out of energy. But Newton's law tells us there must be another force at work.

3. The ball stops because of the force called friction. Friction acts to slow things that are moving. Another word for friction is 'grip'. This is how we think friction works. Moving things slide or run over each other like the football rolls over the grass. While this is happening, the surface (or outside) of the football touches the grass. The surface of the football is fairly smooth to touch but if you could look at it under a microscope you would see it is made of lots of little 'hills and valleys'. The surface of the grass is quite rough even to touch. As these surfaces move over each other, the rough bits catch and slow down the movement. There is also friction as the ball moves through the air.

4. If we slide a flat stone over a frozen pond, it will move a long way before it stops. Both the surfaces are unusually smooth so there is little friction. But cleaning a carpet by brushing it with a stiff brush is hard work. There is a lot of friction between the two rough surfaces. We use a lot of energy to overcome the force of friction made by moving the brush over the carpet. (That is why Mr Hoover invented his carpet cleaner!)

5. Friction is useful. It helps to grip the ground. We wear shoes with gripping soles so we don't slide about. We put moulded rubber tyres on cars so they hold the rough surface of the road. But friction can also be a nuisance. For example, inside car engines, the surfaces of the metal parts move over each other, creating friction. If nothing is done, the force of friction would make the metal get hotter and hotter (like our hands when we rub them together). Hot metal sticks together. When this happens in engines, the car breaks down. We can cut down the friction by using oil to make the metal surfaces slippery. When you ride a bike, you use friction to make you go: the tyres grip on the road surface. You also use friction to stop: the brake pads rub against the wheel rims.

SECTION B: TALKING, THINKING AND LEARNING

QUESTIONING TEXTS

Discuss your group's ideas about each paragraph.

Paragraph 1 Isaac Newton

Words we looked up in the dictionary _____

Three keywords _____ / _____ / _____

Summary in two sentences

a. _____

b. _____

Two questions this paragraph would answer

a. _____
   _____

b. _____
   _____

Paragraph 2 Kicking a ball

Words we looked up in the dictionary _____

Three keywords _____ / _____ / _____

Summary in two sentences

a. _____

b. _____

Two questions this paragraph would answer

a. _____
   _____

b. _____
   _____

Worksheet 12C

Thinking Out Loud   Copyright © 2006 Dawes, Mercer and Wegerif

THINKING OUT LOUD

Worksheet 12C

Paragraph 3 Friction

Words we looked up in the dictionary _____

Three keywords _____ / _____ / _____

Summary in two sentences

a. _____

b. _____

Two questions this paragraph would answer

a. _____

b. _____

Paragraph 4 Mr Hoover

Words we looked up in the dictionary _____

Three keywords _____ / _____ / _____

Summary in two sentences

a. _____

b. _____

Two questions this paragraph would answer

a. _____

b. _____

Paragraph 5 A Useful Nuisance

Words we looked up in the dictionary _____

Three keywords _____ / _____ / _____

Summary in two sentences

a. _____

b. _____

Two questions this paragraph would answer

a. _____

b. _____

SECTION B: TALKING, THINKING AND LEARNING

13. LOOKING INTO POEMS

Resources
Worksheets *13A: Thinking together about poems*
             13B: Two short poems

Aims
- To encourage children to justify opinions with reasons.
- To be able to arrive at a group decision.
- To deepen their understanding and appreciation of poetry.

Whole-class introduction
Explain to the children the aims for Lesson 13. Briefly remind the children of their chosen ground rules for group work. Give each group a copy of Worksheets *13A* and *13B*. Choose children to read aloud the two poems which will be used in the group activity.

Group work
Ask the groups to choose a poem to discuss using the 'Thinking Together' points in *Worksheet 13A* to guide their discussion. Allowing 5–10 minutes for each poem, the groups talk about both poems. The aim of this discussion is to come to an agreement about which piece is the group's favourite, which they like least, and why. Then take one poem at a time and ask groups what they enjoyed or disliked about it. Choose a class favourite poem for display. Alternatively, ask a group at a time to report on their discussion of any one poem. Display the poems, along with the reasons the children have given for liking or disliking them.

Whole-class plenary
Ask the children to reflect on the session content and on the quality of their talk together:
  Did everyone in your group talk about the poems?
  What sort of things can you remember other people saying?

Extension work
Ask the children to each choose a poem from your classroom resources. In their talk groups, they should look at each poem in turn, together, stating what they like about the poems and why, without having to agree on a group favourite. Poems could be displayed with comments such as: 'I liked this poem because…' or 'I did not like this poem because…'

Use the 'talking points' structure to initiate and support group talk about:
- poems
- fiction
- non-fiction
- pictures or paintings
- video.

Thinking together about poems

Choose either poem to start with. Read it together. Now read one 'Thinking Together' point at a time and use the ground rules to talk about it. Try to find out as much about the poems as possible so you can decide which is the group favourite and give a reason for your choice.

Open all the cages—Thinking Together points
The writer likes animals
It would be cruel to let parrots out
The parrots are in the zoo
In the wild, parrots live in rainforests
Birds have an easy life in a cage so don't want to be let out
Rainforests are being cut down so we need to keep some parrots safe in cages
All caged animals should be free to live in the wild
Most parrots can't actually fly
You could put the word 'ideas' instead of 'parrots' and the poem would still make sense
We don't like this poem because
We like this poem because

The sea—Thinking Together points
We can describe a time when we saw the sea
We can picture the sort of dog the sea seems like—we can describe it …
The clashing teeth and shaggy jaws are like—which bits of the sea …
The sea changes. The poem shows a picture of the sea at three different times
The sea makes many different sounds—this poem reminds you of some
Even fierce dogs look gentle when they are asleep
You can put the word 'sea-lion' instead of 'dog' and the poem still makes sense: would any other animal do? Cat, horse, elephant, mouse?
We don't like this poem because
We like this poem because

SECTION B: TALKING, THINKING AND LEARNING

TWO SHORT POEMS

Open All the Cages

Open all the cages,
Let the parrots fly –
Green and gold and purple parrots
Streaming up the sky.

Open all the cages,
Let the parrots out
Screeching, squawking
         parrots swooping
Happily about.

Open all the cages,
Set the parrots free –
Flocks of parrots
         flapping homewards
South across the sea.

Silent trees in silent forests
Long for parrots, so –
Open all the cages,
Let the parrots go!

© Richard Edwards from *Moon Frog*
(Walker Books)

The Sea

The sea is a hungry dog,
Giant and grey.
He rolls on the beach all day.
With his clashing teeth and shaggy jaws
Hour upon hour he gnaws
The rumbling, tumbling stones,
And 'Bones, bones, bones, bones!'
The giant sea-dog moans,
Licking his greasy paws.

And when the night wind roars
And the moon rocks in the stormy cloud,
He bounds to his feet and sniffs and sniffs,
Shaking his wet sides over the cliffs,
And howls and hollos long and loud.

But on quiet days in May or June,
When even the grasses on the dune
Play no more their reedy tune,
With his head between his paws
He lies on the sandy shores,
So quiet, so quiet he scarcely snores.

©James Reeves, from *Complete Poems for Children*
(Heinemann) Reprinted by permission of the James
Reeves estate

Worksheet 13B

THINKING OUT LOUD

14. STAYING FRIENDS

Resources
Worksheets   *14A: Staying friends* (a story: one copy per group)
14B: Thinking together about staying friends

Aims
- To use the ground rules to discuss social and moral issues.
- To deepen understanding of two citizenship issues: personal morality and bullying.

Whole-class introduction
Explain to the children the aims for Lesson 14. Choose fluent readers to read a paragraph each of the story aloud from *Worksheet 14A*.

Group work
When the class has heard the story, ask the groups to discuss a story ending together using their agreed ground rules for talk. Use *Worksheet 14B* to structure the discussion. Ask each group to read out their story ending, giving reasons for their choices.

Whole-class plenary
Ask the children to reflect on the content of the session, and on the quality of their talk together:
Did you remember to use the ground rules for talk? Can you give an example?
If you worked with different people, would you still be able to use the ground rules?

Extension work
The class can further discuss the citizenship issues raised by the story, giving opinions on topics such as:

- friendship
- keeping secrets
- what is 'right' and 'wrong'
- why people choose to do things that they know are 'wrong'
- bullying—girls and boys.

The children could present and display their stories in written or cartoon form. Alternatively, they could act out the entire story as a play.

SECTION B: TALKING, THINKING AND LEARNING

STAYING FRIENDS

Charlie, Abi and Joe did everything together. They were best friends and everyone knew they were. Charlie and Joe got together one day to talk about what they were going to give Abi for her birthday. It was recess at school, so they only had a few moments to talk before Abi came along.

"I've already got Abi a present, but it's a secret," said Joe.

"What is it?" asked Charlie. "Go on, you can tell me."

"But it's a secret," Joe repeated. "You know—something you don't tell anybody."

"Huh, you can tell your friends secrets," said Charlie. "That's the point of having friends. People you can trust. I bet you haven't got a present at all, that's why you won't tell."

"I have! So there," said Joe, "but…"

"I know, I know. It's a big secret. Well. I've got a secret too and I won't tell it to you unless you tell me about the present," said Charlie, a bit crossly.

"Well," said Joe reluctantly, "you must promise not to tell. It's important to me. I'm not sure you've got a secret at all."

But Charlie had. "That's all you know," said Charlie. "Listen, I promise. I'll tell mine first. And you promise too."

"I promise," said Joe, giving in.

"I've got a packet of lollies in my coat pocket!" whispered Charlie. That certainly was a secret, because no one was allowed lollies in school. Charlie proved it by showing Joe a corner of the packet. "I'm going to eat them at lunchtime. You can share."

"No! You idiot! You'll get into trouble."

"Not a chance. I'm going to go right in the corner of the oval. The teachers never go that far."

"You're crazy then," Joe told him. "Someone's bound to tell on you. Not me, I mean, because I promised. But someone will see you, and I bet they'll tell."

Charlie shrugged. "I can get away with it, easy. Hey, now your turn—you have to tell me what you've got for Abi."

"Oh, all right, then," said Joe. He leaned closer and whispered, "An electronic buzzer for her bike!"

"Wow," said Charlie. Then they saw Abi running across the playground towards them, and they quickly started a game of tag.

Charlie's plan for lunchtime was to take a book and pretend to read in the corner of the oval. Everyone would think he didn't want to be disturbed, and he could munch away quite happily behind the cover. It worked really well and he'd eaten most of the lollies, when he was annoyed to spot Abi running across the oval towards him.

"What's up with you?" she called.

"Go away! Can't you see I'm trying to read in peace?" he called back, but she came over and he hastily stuffed the packet back into his pocket.

"What do you mean, trying to read? That's a joke—you have to be forced to pick up a book in the classroom," she said.

"Well I've decided to try harder," said Charlie. It didn't sound very convincing.

Worksheet 14A

Thinking Out Loud   Copyright © 2006 Dawes, Mercer and Wegerif   81

Abi took a good look at him. "Hmmm!" she said. "Your mouth is a sort of greeny-black colour. Anyone would think you were over here eating lollies!" She laughed and Charlie had to laugh too, in a guilty sort of way, and they both looked around to see who was nearby. But everyone else was playing football, doing cartwheels, or just running about.

"Are you going to tell on me?"

"Me?" said Abi, "No. I can keep a secret." Charlie held out the sweets for her to take one, but she shook her head.

"I can keep secrets too," said Charlie. "And I know something you don't know."

"Oh be quiet!" said Abi. "You always think you know everything. You shouldn't be such a show-off."

"Well I do know something, so there, and it's about you."

Abi was a bit surprised by this, and quite interested. "Go on, tell me then," she said.

"It's a secret—I promised not to," Charlie replied.

"See. You're just making things up as usual."

Charlie got quite cross again. "If you must know, it's about your birthday," he said. "Joe told me what present he got you."

Abi smiled, and got up to go. "You definitely mustn't tell me then. I love surprises! I'm off— I don't want to be in trouble like you."

She ran away and Charlie stuffed four of the lollies into his mouth and chewed hard. Somehow it didn't seem so much fun. And then, from nowhere it seemed, Lucas Jones appeared beside him. Lucas had a horrible expression, a mixture of being pleased and very, very mean. "Hello there Charlie. Enjoying your book?" said Lucas, sitting down, far too close.

Charlie's mouth was too full to answer, but it didn't matter because he didn't know what to say anyway. He felt a wild, panicky feeling. He would have liked to run away, but where to, with a sticky, chewy mouthful of lollies?

"Going to share them with me? Then I might not tell." Lucas laughed nastily.

Charlie dug hopelessly in his pocket and came out with the empty packet. "Gone," he mumbled, trying to swallow.

"I'd better tell, then," said Lucas. "Miss!" The teacher didn't seem to hear.

Charlie dragged on Lucas's arm, imagining what would happen at home if he were caught. "Shhh! Don't tell. Don't," said Charlie.

"Why not? Got any money? No? Anything else? I might be very kind and not tell, but then what are you going to give me in return, hey?" Lucas managed to look even more unpleasant. "I know—what were you and Joe whispering about at recess? I saw you. You'd better tell me," he said, pinching Charlie's arm. "I bet it was something about me."

"Don't be stupid," said Charlie, wishing all of a sudden that the teacher was nearer. "He was telling me about his new computer game."

Lucas hit him once, hard. "Liar! Tell me. Or I'll tell on you. This is your last chance."

"I can't tell; it was a secret, and I promised," said Charlie in a panic. Why didn't the bell go? What could he say next? What would happen now?

SECTION B: TALKING, THINKING AND LEARNING

THINKING TOGETHER ABOUT 'STAYING FRIENDS'

Think together about the Staying Friends story

Decide who is going to do the writing for all of you.
Use the Ground Rules for Talk to discuss your ideas about each section of this worksheet.
Try to reach a group decision.

Our ideas about Staying Friends

Think of three good describing words for each of the main characters.

Joe	Abi
Charlie	Lucas

Think together to decide on three different things Charlie could do as the story ends.

1

2

3

Which is your favourite, and why?

Number   because…

Is Lucas a boy or a girl? How do you know?

Boy or girl?   because…

Now talk about a SHORT ending for the story. Remember to ask everyone for their ideas and talk about what would make the most interesting ending before deciding. Write down your agreed ending.

Worksheet 14B

Thinking Out Loud   Copyright © 2006 Dawes, Mercer and Wegerif

THINKING OUT LOUD

15. STRATEGY

Resources
1 cm squared paper, pencils, rubbers, ruler, one counter or coin per group; *Hurkle* software on the Thinking Together website: www.thinkingtogether.org.uk

Aims
- To encourage collaboration in pairs.
- To accept group responsibility for decisions.
- To introduce grid references and co-ordinates.
- To apply the ground rules to problem solving in mathematics.

Whole-class introduction
Explain that children are paired to work with others in fours. Explain the grid system or the co-ordinate system that will be used. Introduce the version of the game you are using, stressing that the point is to talk together in order to discover the best strategy for finding the Hurkle in as few turns as possible.

Group work
Children are paired. Groups consist of two pairs. Each pair draws two grids on squared paper. The grids have the letters A to J along the bottom and the numbers 1 to 10 along the left-hand side. (If you want to use this to introduce co-ordinate work use numbers on both axes and refer to the bottom as horizontal or 'x' and the left side as vertical or 'y'.) To prepare for play, one member of each pair must first position their counter (or 'Hurkle') on one grid. This completed grid must be kept hidden.

Each pair then has to try to find the Hurkle by guessing which square it is in. Each pair starts with a blank grid and their own completed grid. Toss a coin to decide which pair starts. The starting pair decides on and chooses a square using conventional grid referencing, for example, square G8. The opposing team has to reveal whether the Hurkle is in that square or not and add the following information:

>   VERSION 1: how far away the Hurkle is, counting each square up or along sideways as one square
>   VERSION 2: whether the Hurkle is or is not within three squares of the guessed square
>   VERSION 3: the direction that the Hurkle is to be found, for example: right-hand east (assuming the top of the grid to be north) and so on. Double references, for example, NE or SW, are only to be given if the Hurkle is directly diagonal to the guessed square.

Play the game enough times for the children to experiment with strategies—at least three times or more depending on how much time you have available.

SECTION B: TALKING, THINKING AND LEARNING

Whole-class plenary

Ask the groups of four which strategy was most effective. Ask them to explain their reasons to the class, using a large grid drawn on a blackboard or whiteboard. Ask for comments and discussion. Draw out the mathematical elements involved. In each version there is an optimum strategy and in each version it is different:

IN VERSION 1: the optimum strategy is to guess two different points and then work out the intersections of the two circles which centre on each point, and have a radius of the distance given at each point.

IN VERSION 2: a good strategy is to design a search pattern, keeping three squares from the edge and three squares from the last guess. Once within the area, three squares from the Hurkle, it is necessary to then draw an imaginary circle of possible squares (three around the near guess), avoiding any squares within three squares of previous failed guesses, and then select a square within the designated area and repeat this procedure.

IN VERSION 3: a good strategy is to start in a middle square, draw an imaginary line from the guessed square to the edge of the grid in the direction given, then place the next guess counter exactly half-way along this line. This strategy can be repeated indefinitely. The children may discover alternative strategies, using this version.

Ask the children to reflect on the session content and on the quality of their talk together:
Did talking to each other help you to work out a strategy? How?

Extension work

- Children can prepare grids to use with someone at home.
- This lesson could be followed by work on adding and subtracting co-ordinates.
- Other games can be played collaboratively in order to help children work as a team and minimise the conflict brought about by assigning 'blame' to individuals when things go wrong. Computer-based adventure programs may also be useful when approached in this way. Draughts, dominoes, and other board games which involve an element of choice as well as chance can be used to support collaborative discussion between pairs of children.

THINKING OUT LOUD

16. ICT AND LEARNING CONVERSATIONS

In a talk-focused classroom, the use of ICT (Information and Communications Technology) provides teachers and learners with access to a comprehensive range of useful resources for discussion. There is great potential for learning when children use the tools of spoken language together with the tools of ICT. Applying the ground rules for talk can help children working in groups at the computer to spend time thinking aloud together to solve curriculum-related problems. Group decisions based on discussion of ideas and reasons are more likely to lead to successful outcomes and deeper learning. This way of working enables groups to do better, and learn more, than when choices are made by individuals on impulse. This section indicates how ICT can be used to help generate such learning conversations.

1. Structuring the lesson

The three-part lesson structure advocated throughout this book provides opportunities for productive talk at the computer and during introductory and plenary sessions.

Example: Using ICT to generate learning conversations in the context of making a PowerPoint presentation about the Antarctic to show at a parents' evening

AIMS

To find out about wildlife and human life in a polar climate. As a group, to collect and order information, making decisions about relevance, sequencing, appropriate vocabulary and presentation.

WHOLE-CLASS INTRODUCTION

Explain the aims of the lesson; ask children to recall their ground rules for talk. Provide information about (a) ICT skills required (b) information sources.

GROUP WORK

Preparation of PowerPoint presentations.

WHOLE-CLASS PLENARY

Ask the groups to show their presentations, explaining to the class what material they have incorporated and why. Ask the groups to evaluate their group work. How well did your group work together? Who offered ideas? Were there opposing points of view? Did the ground rules for talk help discussion? If not, how should they be adapted?

---

2. Choosing curriculum software

A curriculum software package may claim to support group work. It might, if the software is challenging and motivating, but might not if children are unaware of the importance of speaking and listening for their own learning and that of others. Using jointly-agreed ground

rules reduces the element of chance and increases the probability that learning conversations will take place. There are some general features of software that do help children to work together productively. Software should provide:
- Sufficiently complex and meaningful problems—choices must matter.
- On-screen discussion prompts such as 'Talk together to decide'; 'What does the group think?' and so on. These act as cues for Exploratory Talk. However, children who have not undertaken talk lessons may ignore such prompts.
- Information with varying levels of difficulty and complexity.
- Discouragement for turn taking or beating the clock, both of which hamper efforts to share ideas.
- Scenarios which encourage role-play and narrative.
- A minimum of typed input. Searching for letters effectively halts discussion. Multi-choice answers help to ensure a focus on the curriculum topic.

3. Organising group talk at the computer

Before work begins, ask each group to take decisions about who is going to sit where, who will use the mouse and so on. Ensure that a list of the class ground rules for talk is visible from the computer. For example, ask each child to write a rule on a post-it note and stick these around the screen. Refer to these rules and their purpose in introductions and plenaries. During group work, ask one child from each group to visit a different group and look at what they are doing, listen to the discussion, and report back. Use the plenary to check how useful or interesting this practice was. If computers are networked, ask one group to show their work, explain their reasoning, and talk about how everyone has contributed.

Use targeted intervention to help you to include those finding it difficult to express their ideas, to offer suggestions, and to model Exploratory Talk. For example you might:
- Summarise what has been said.
- Ask questions that encourage contributions.
- Try to create conditions in which less confident group members can contribute.
- Remind groups that the quality of their talk is as important as other outcomes.
- Point out ideas the group has generated that may have been difficult for individuals to achieve alone.
- Remain with the group until they can continue their discussion without your support.
- Try to encourage the group to ask one another questions.

4. Reflection on own learning

At the end of the lesson, provide each individual with a copy of page 88: *Thinking Out Loud Reflection on Own Learning*. Allow children thinking time to complete this, and retain as a record or for discussion of individual learning targets.

THINKING OUT LOUD

Lesson 16

THINKING OUT LOUD
REFLECTION ON OWN LEARNING

What have I learnt and how did I learn it?

Aims of the lesson:

My personal study goal:

Joint study goal for our group:

What I learnt was:

I learned by:

Reading	☐	Writing	☐
Speaking and listening	☐	Watching	☐
An activity	☐	Investigation	☐
Role-play	☐	ICT use	☐
Whole-class discussion	☐	Group discussion	☐

The most useful of these was:

I liked/disliked this part of the lesson:

Because:

I supported the learning of others by:

Advantages of learning in a group were:

Difficulties in group work and how to sort them out:

My next personal study goal is:

SECTION B: TALKING, THINKING AND LEARNING

TALK CERTIFICATES

A certificate is a good means of emphasising to children what they have achieved in their efforts to talk and think together. A suggested format appears on the next page. However, the children might also like to design their own.

> **The Thinking Together Website**
> - Don't forget that you can access the Thinking Together website at the following address: www.thinkingtogether.org.uk

THINKING OUT LOUD

Talk Lesson Certificate

This is to certify that

_____

has been part of a talk group
and learnt how to discuss
before deciding.

Members of my group:

Talk Lesson Certificate

This is to certify that

_____

has been part of a talk group
and learnt how to discuss
before deciding.

Members of my group: